MARGARET THATCHER
THE FIRST TEN YEARS

MARGARET THATCHER
THE FIRST TEN YEARS
Lady Olga Maitland

Photographs by
Srdja Djukanovic

Sidgwick & Jackson London

First published in Great Britain in 1989 by

Sidgwick & Jackson Limited

1 Tavistock Chambers, Bloomsbury Way

London WC1A 2SG

ISBN 0 283 99831 8

Photoset by Rowland Phototypesetting Limited

Bury St Edmunds, Suffolk

Art Direction & Book Design by Bob Hook

Printed and bound in Great Britain by

Butler & Tanner Ltd, Frome and London

CONTENTS

INTRODUCTION

On 4 May 1989, flowers, congratulations and tributes flowed into No. 10 Downing Street. All day the famous shiny black door of No. 10 opened and shut to well-wishers celebrating a decade of Mrs Margaret Thatcher's premiership. Prime Minister and First Lord of the Treasury, her standing is higher than that of any Prime Minister since the war. She is known all over the world, from Lima to Beijing, and she is a fêted figure in Washington and Moscow. No wonder; she has been elected Prime Minister three consecutive times – the first to do so since Lord Liverpool held office from 1812 to 1827. She has left her stamp not only on domestic politics but on international affairs worldwide.

At the last Conservative Party Conference in Brighton, a rapturous 4000-member party faithful cheered the Prime Minister to the rooftops. They clapped for a full nine minutes, singing 'Ten More Years' and dancing in the aisles. The atmosphere was exuberant and confident – a far cry from the feeling ten years ago when Britain was plunged into a demoralized gloom, unable to lift up her head in the face of the troubles that beset the nation. There was near anarchy from strikes nationwide. Television screens showed picketers at hospital gates, making life or death decisions for patients; the dead lay unburied; and refuse piled up in the streets for rats to prey on. And through all this the then Prime Minister, James Callaghan, returned from an overseas trip to the Caribbean to say, 'Crisis? What crisis?'

Today that is a dim and distant nightmare. There is a new word in the English language: 'Thatcherism'. It depicts a remarkable revolution. No other Prime Minister has had such an adjective ascribed to his name. Thatcherism has meant rolling back the state controls and having faith in the common man to take his *own* decisions. Thatcherism has given every man and woman an incentive to take care of himself or herself and his or her family. It encourages prosperity through enterprise – a word that became a keynote in her revolution. Margaret Thatcher's policy of selling off state interests – de-nationalizing them to the private sector to give healthy competition and wider choice – made a fundamental change to the whole framework of society.

It could be fairly said that she is a radical revolutionary and unique because what she said she would do she did! She fulfilled her promises where all previous governments had failed.

She surprised her foes by sticking to her philosophy – there were no 'U' turns when the going got rough. Her philosophy is based on conviction rather than the political expediency of the day. In hindsight no one should have been surprised at her stand. In 1968 she gave a lecture at the Blackpool Conservative Party Conference, setting out her beliefs. She has never wavered from them.

Out of a conviction based on gut instinct grew her policies for Victorian values: the importance of sustaining family life; the emphasis on reward for hard work; and

Prime Minister Margaret Thatcher in her study at No. 10 Downing Street. November 1988.

the need to care for others in the prosperity that ensued. As the decade unravelled it became obvious just how unique she has been – insistent upon taking tough decisions and oblivious to unpopularity when she felt the final result would be worth it. Mrs Margaret Thatcher is unique for having the courage – although often totally alone in the world, with even her own Cabinet critical of her – to push through an economic policy of tough restraint which turned the tide for Britain. With prosperity, Britain has again become a country to be reckoned with. Economic power has bought influence; Britain's economic miracle and privatization programme has been copied the world over. Even Moscow sends its businessmen to learn new techniques.

On the world stage Mrs Thatcher's voice rings out – often controversially; but, whatever reaction she causes, it could never be said that she is ignored or accused of representing a country of little note. Today Europe pays attention. A few years back the Kremlin called her the 'Iron Lady'; now she is the most admired premier in the world.

A visionary indeed, Mrs Thatcher positively glows with the trappings of office. The cares and impossibly long days have made her blossom while all her predecessors have wilted within a few short years, developing puffy eyes and paunches. Illness dogged them all. Margaret Thatcher is as healthy and vibrant as she has ever been. She has thrived in a country that has thrived on her, bringing promise and praise to Britain, which once more plays a leading role on the world stage.

CHAPTER ONE
WHERE IT BEGAN

Ten years ago, on 4 May 1979, Britain wondered and marvelled at the election of Britain's first woman Prime Minister. For Margaret Thatcher that great day had begun more than twenty-four hours earlier. The campaign base had been Mrs Thatcher's Chelsea home in Flood Street. On Wednesday 2 May the team gathered for supper. Present were her husband Denis, her daughter Carol, Gordon Reece and David Wolfson. Gordon, always quick off the mark, had the latest Fleet Street polls in his hand. They were discouraging – Labour was one point ahead. The question was: who should tell Margaret?

Supper was eaten in an ominous silence as Carol started taking bets on the final outcome.

'Mummy, what do you think the final majority will be?'

'Forty' was the reply. The stomachs of the assembled company chilled and Mrs Thatcher was told that the latest poll placed her one point behind Neil Kinnock. There was a pregnant pause before she said, 'I don't believe that.'

On election day, Thursday 3 May, Margaret Thatcher followed the customary itinerary of MPs – she toured the constituency in Finchley, visiting the polling stations and chatting to supporters. Finally, confident of a reasonable majority, she returned home to Flood Street, to begin what amounted to an agonizing thirty-six-hour wait before she could be formally announced as the new Prime Minister.

Pacing has never been Mrs Thatcher's style. To while away the hours before she returned to Finchley for the count, she nervously re-organized the drawers of her desk. Bits of paper flew feverishly into the wastepaper basket. After supper, she was off with Carol and Denis to Finchley Town Hall for the final count. The tension was too much for her agent Roy Langston and the party officials. They set up a television in a side room to monitor the results as they came in. The first results were not that promising – there was a recount in Peterborough and another good seat was looking uncertain.

Then, finally, came a bustle of activity in the hall outside and the mayor gathered up his notes. Mrs Thatcher, and the other candidates, moved to the microphones at the centre of the stage. Her results were announced – she had a majority of 7900, and the television screen was heralding more votes as they came pouring in thick and fast. At the Conservative headquarters in Smith Square the rest of the team were glued to television sets. Gordon Reece, large cigar in his hand as always, was predicting a majority of sixty. Margaret and Denis arrived at 3 a.m. As they entered the building

Celebrations for Margaret Thatcher's election victory. A bodyguard congratulates the new Prime Minister.

Margaret Thatcher leaves Central Office for her new home at Downing Street.

a great roar of approval was sounded by the crowds outside. Inside, all of the Party workers herded to the stairs and the hall to welcome her, and the room flashed with photographers' lightbulbs. She spotted the comfortable, uncle-like figure of her speech writer – playwright Sir Ronald Millar.

'Oh, do you think it is going to be all right?' she asked uncertainly.

'I bloody know it's going to be all right.'

The results continued to come in as Margaret and Denis nervously watched. Others were already celebrating with the champagne that had been thoughtfully provided by Gordon Reece. But for the Party Leader herself the tension was almost unbearable – she hardly sipped. The media, however, avidly tucked into the 800 cans of beer brought in to keep them solvent. The figures were good.

At 4 a.m. Margaret turned to Ronnie Millar. 'Have you thought . . . if we win, have you thought of anything I could say at Downing Street?'

'Yes,' he said, and together they sought a quiet room where he followed his usual custom. He pulled a piece of paper out of his pocket and read it aloud to her – it was a quotation from St Francis of Assisi: 'Where there is discord may we bring harmony, where there is error may we bring truth, where there is doubt may we bring fact, and where there is despair may we bring hope.'

For the first time, she allowed the emotion to swell up and her eyes filled with tears. Perhaps it was then that the reality of becoming Prime Minister hit her for the first time. The first congratulations came via a telephone call from Australia – Premier Malcolm Fraser was on the line. Mrs Thatcher cautiously thanked him. Anything could happen and she still did not know what kind of majority it would be.

Finally, at 5 a.m., they headed back to Flood Street. The group of well-wishers had become a crowd – bedecked with blue ribbons – as they waved flags, chanted and sang. The cheering went on until well past dawn. And there was no sleep that night – her family reported that Margaret sat up making telephone calls.

That Friday was as long and drawn out as Election Day. Indeed, the first half of that day was perhaps the most nerve-wracking of the entire campaign. Margaret Thatcher could not be Prime Minister until Jim Callaghan had tendered his resignation to the Queen at Buckingham Palace. At this point Mrs Thatcher would be summoned by the Queen and officially asked to form a government. Only then could she face the world's press and officially take possession of No. 10 Downing Street.

By mid-morning there was really no point in remaining at Flood Street, and Margaret and Denis drove to the Central Office where celebrations had reached a high peak. The champagne was flowing, and amidst the high spirits and laughter a vast, hastily cooked chocolate cake in the shape of the door at No. 10 was presented to her. 'Margaret's Success Story' was written in icing across the top of the cake, and Mrs Thatcher was warm in her thanks to everyone who had devotedly supported her.

The previous night's celebrations gradually took their toll and, exhausted, everyone drifted away. Margaret set down to work again with Ronnie Millar on the acceptance speech to be made outside No. 10. Packing up and moving in was already under way.

The Thatcher family sat like an island in the middle of the sea of boxes and moving equipment. Only Ronnie Millar, at the insistence of Margaret, stayed by their side. They pecked listlessly at a cold lunch sent up from the canteen and waited in the now barren office for the summons from Buckingham Palace. The clock ticked on. The air was heavy with anticipation. Carol Thatcher remembers fidgeting while Denis dozed and Mark stared aimlessly. Margaret sat straight in her chair, obviously nervous. Ronnie Millar noted that she was pre-occupied, uncertain of how to get to Buckingham Palace and back without meeting Mr Callaghan who would pass through the same route. His headquarters at Transport House were, after all, just across the road from the Central Office.

Ronnie reassured her, amused that she should be concerned. 'It's all right. You won't find yourselves glaring at each other as you pass.'

And so the company again lapsed into silence. When would the call from Buckingham Palace come? They were suddenly rewarded – the telephone rang loudly in the room and for a moment everyone was frozen. *Wrong number*! It was a full five minutes later before it shrilled again, and Mrs Thatcher's secretary Caroline Stevens answered it from the next room. 'Edward Heath would like to offer his congratulations,' she said solemnly.

There was a long pause, then steadily Margaret said, 'Would you thank him very much.' She was too tense to speak to him – perhaps later. . . .

The room was thick with silence. The telephone rang again.

'This is it,' declared Caroline for the second time that day.

'Yes, yes, just one moment.' She returned to the room. 'Sir Philip Moore (the Queen's Secretary) would like to speak to you.'

Margaret calmly stood.

'Good afternoon, Sir Philip.' Her voice carried from the next room. 'This is Margaret Thatcher speaking.' The ensuing words were denied a public hearing –

Opposite, Margaret Thatcher greets the press for the first time as Prime Minister outside No. 10 Downing Street.

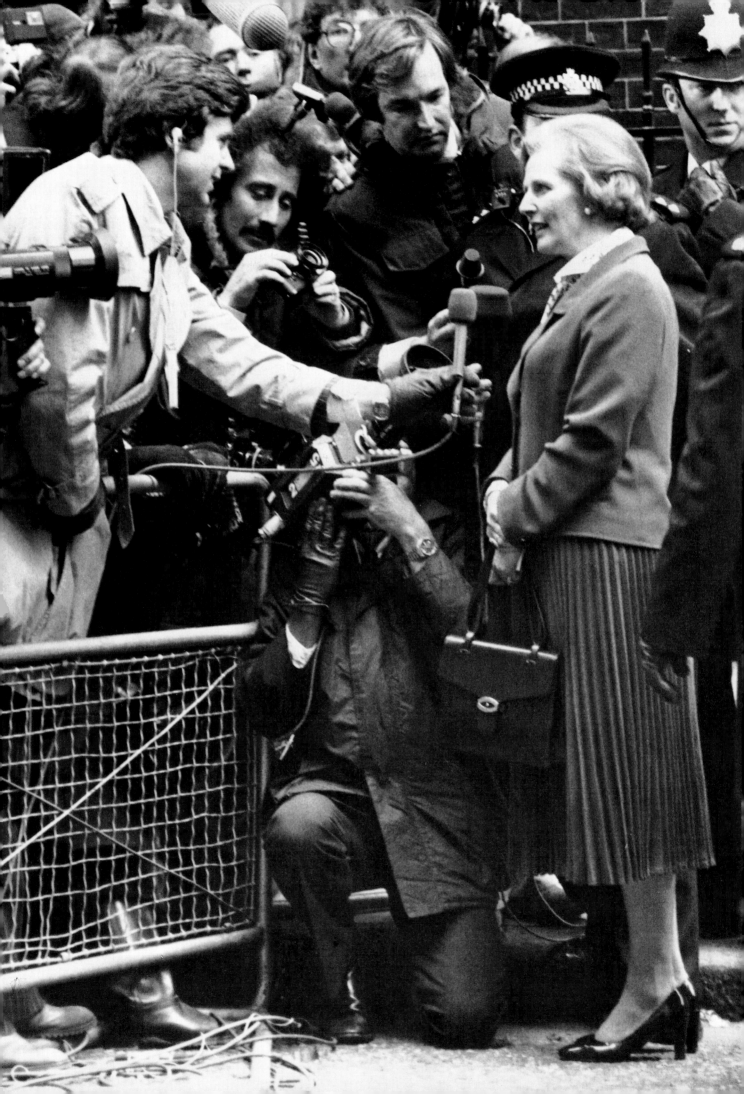

with all the grace she could muster, Margaret Thatcher closed the door leaving her audience in silence. Minutes later she was back. 'Right,' she said crisply. 'We're off.'

At 2.45 p.m. a car drove Denis and Margaret up the Mall, round the Victoria Statue and in through the right-hand privy purse entrance to Buckingham Palace. They were greeted at once. Denis was entertained by Palace aides in a reception room downstairs, while his wife was escorted along the red-carpeted corridors, lined with heavy oil paintings, engravings and statues, to take the lift to the first floor. She met with the Queen in her study – it was a success, lasting just over forty-five minutes. There had been much speculation about how these two very dedicated and influential women – then both fifty-three – would get on.

Enthusiasts were disappointed to find they did not kick off their shoes and enter into a feminine tête-à-tête. Prime Minister Mrs Margaret Thatcher curtsied at the door; at the greeting and again at her departure. It was a formal occasion marking the respect that the two women had for one another – respect that has been maintained throughout the decade. Their conversation will never be made public and Mrs Thatcher has deeply respected the confidence. It was, however, reported by a senior member of the Queen's staff, Michael Shea, later in her term of office, that the Queen was critical of the effects of monetarism – and the methods to attain economic recovery. Their relationship has always been businesslike but the criticism hurt.

When the meeting ended she collected Denis and they set off for No. 10, now legitimately her new home. It is a house that has seen history enter and leave it for every day of its existence but never before had it welcomed a female Prime Minister. The car nosed its way into Downing Street which was alive with cheering supporters. Press from around the world clamoured for exclusives, while thousands of well-wishers burst into an enthusiastic rendition of 'For She's a Jolly Good Fellow'.

Prime Minister Mrs Thatcher stood on the steps of her new home, framed by the famous black door with its bright brass fittings, and confidently recited St Francis of Assisi. With pride shining in her eyes she added, 'To all the British people, howsoever they may have voted, may I say this: now that the election is over, may we get together and strive to serve and strengthen the country of which we are so proud to be a part.' She went on to pledge 'I shall strive unceasingly to try to fulfil the trust and confidence the British people have put in me.

'And finally one last thing; in the words of Airey Neave, whom we had hoped to bring here with us, "Now there is work to be done."'

The crowd surged with excitement as Margaret Thatcher turned to enter No. 10 – her attention already focused on the next detail on her itinerary. She prepared to form a Government.

That night she sat alone at her desk in her first-floor study. Not only was she the first female Prime Minister, but also she had won the election with the largest swing to Conservative, and with the largest majority of votes since the war.

Previous page, **P**ressmen gather for the arrival of victorious Margaret Thatcher. *Opposite,* Flowers from well-wishers arriving at Downing Street.

CHAPTER TWO
THE EARLY YEARS

Had the Prime Minister taken the time to pause and reflect as she walked into the black and white marble hall of No. 10 – flanked by portraits of the first Prime Minister Hugh Walpole – and up the graceful stairs to her first-floor study, she would have remembered how it all began.

Some say that politicians are born lucky. To a degree luck must play its part; but luck alone cannot possibly account for the steely determination and sense of mission that has always characterized Margaret Thatcher.

She was born Margaret Hilda Roberts on 13 October 1925 in an upstairs room above the grocer's shop her parents owned in Grantham, Lincolnshire. Grantham is a market town with some industry, although it remains quiet and perhaps most typical of hard-working 'middle England'. Margaret's parents, Alf and Beatrice Roberts, were unpretentious, diligent people who had rigorously built their lives around the Methodist church. Home life was simple but not spartan. It was, however, dedicated to the work ethos that 'If a job is worth doing, it is worth doing well'. To this end, there was no time for frivolity; every spare moment was devoted to study or to helping others through the church. Margaret developed her first taste of politics as a child through helping her father in his political campaigns as a town councillor – he eventually became mayor.

Alf Roberts was the centre of Margaret's life and she adored him. Having left school at the age of fourteen, he'd never had the opportunity to study as his daughter did. He was, however, a keenly intelligent man, eager to learn, and passed on this enthusiasm to his daughter. They also shared the same restless energy and deep conviction towards right and wrong. Margaret Roberts's childhood was happy but not, perhaps, fun-filled – home life was taken seriously in the Roberts's household and money was not available for frivolity. She did well at school, first at the Huntingtower Road Elementary School and then on a minor county scholarship to the Kesteven and Grantham Girls School. She is remembered as being a quiet, pretty girl who was perhaps a shade too serious and immaculate – in her teens she always carried a tiny powder compact, a gift from her sister, and was extremely conscious of her appearance at all times. She consistently headed her class academically, a reflection of the tremendous hard work and application she afforded. Articulate through years of intellectual development encouraged by her father, Margaret showed precosity when questioning visiting speakers at school lectures, indications of her remarkable maturity – even as a youth. She would often begin her questions with a somewhat parliamentary style: 'Does the Speaker. . .'. Her friends gritted their teeth in embarrassment!

The shop that Margaret's father owned; the flat above was her home for most of her childhood years.

Undaunted and unsympathetic to less sensible colleagues, Margaret Roberts ploughed her way through her academic career, setting her heart on attaining a place at Somerville College, Oxford, where she read chemistry. Before she went up to Oxford, she attended elocution lessons to polish the edges of her Lincolnshire accent – a conscious effort to improve herself in every possible aspect. At Oxford she appeared somewhat gauche in her commitment to the Conservative cause, at a time when it was distinctly unfashionable. Margaret's earnestness and dedication succeeded in masking her natural charm and charisma. She did, however, leave her mark on the Oxford University Conservative Association culminating a successful career to become their President.

Most of her social life and energies were applied in this direction. It was during one vacation at home in Grantham with a group of young friends over a late night cocoa that one said, 'You know, I think you would really like to be a Member of Parliament.' Thoughtfully Margaret agreed. Perhaps these innocent words crystallized her personal ambitions – rudiments of which had been forming in her mind for quite some time. Her first priority, on coming down from Oxford with a solid second class degree in Chemistry, was to get a career going. Money was an essential element in providing for a political life – MPs were paid considerably less than today.

The first job she acquired was with BX Plastics Limited – a manufacturing company based near Colchester, Essex – as a research chemist at a salary of £350 a year. Taking up digs nearby, Margaret settled in, and if she may not have become 'one of the lads' she did get along well with her fellow technicians. Her real life, however, began at weekends. She joined the local Colchester Conservative Association and spent every spare moment entrenching herself in politics, energetically travelling from one political conference, debate or function to another.

A chance meeting with the Chairman of the Dartford Conservative Association at a Conservative Party Conference led her to apply to become the Prospective Parliamentary Candidate. It was a solid Labour seat with a majority of over 23,000 in Dartford, Kent. At the age of only twenty-three Margaret beat twenty applicants and was selected.

Margaret Roberts's life was on the move, in more ways than one. She met Denis Thatcher for the first time at her adoption meeting. He had been brought along as a 'spare' man to even numbers for dinner. The meeting was a success and he offered to drive Margaret up to Liverpool Street to catch her train back to Colchester. To the excited twenty-three-year-old, he was perfect. Denis Thatcher was tall, good looking and athletic. Being ten years older than Margaret, he had worldliness which served as a foil to her youth, and further, he was a successful businessman in his own right with a snazzy car and a Chelsea flat.

His previous, albeit brief, war-time marriage had been dissolved, and despite her Methodist background, Margaret chose to ignore it. The subject was never a topic of discussion until a fateful day in 1974 when she became Leader of the Conservative Party and the news broke that the first Mrs Thatcher had become Lady Hickman. Margaret was not at all pleased to hear it discussed.

Margaret's first campaign was enjoyable: for a start she was for the first time in her natural element. The fact that she had a platform and was acknowledged as the Prospective Parliamentary Candidate initiated a tremendous wave of energy, enthusiasm and, above all, sheer hard work. There was nothing she would not attempt, nor was there a limit to the hours she could work. It was a pattern which was to be the hallmark for the future. A German journalist who, out of curiosity, followed her campaign reported: '. . . she was fearless at meetings and pleasant, but cool to meet; blinkered, determined, ambitious.'

She led a deliberately high-profile campaign, capturing the attention of the press. Honing her communication skills to a fine point, she managed to reduce the Labour majority by 1000 on that polling day in February 1950. More importantly, however, she was launched onto the General Election ladder, and eighteen months later, in September 1951, she fought for the seat again. The campaign was much the same as her earlier attempt, but one new element made it a period for Margaret to remember. Just before polling day the news leaked out that Miss Margaret Roberts was engaged to be married to Mr Denis Thatcher.

They were married six weeks later on a bitterly cold December day at a leading Methodist church – Wesley's Chapel in City Road, London; and a beautifully arranged reception at the home of millionaire Sir Alfred Bossom in Carlton Gardens behind Pall Mall followed. He was a great Conservative supporter. It was a honeymoon to remember – Denis whirled his bride off on a holiday that combined business and pleasure with stops in Portugal, Madeira and Paris. It was Margaret's first trip abroad. Home was a Chelsea flat where they shared the first few precious years of private married life.

Top, **C**hoosing the Sunday joint. Margaret Thatcher has continued to shop and cook for her family throughout her career. *Bottom*, Margaret Thatcher at her local grocer in Chelsea, 1979.

Margaret set out to learn how to cook and to indulge in home decorating – a project which became a great source of relaxation. There was never any suggestion that she would be a full-time house-bound wife, and Margaret's first ambition was to study for the Bar to become a barrister. If anyone had any doubts about her determination to keep up the pace, he had only to read the article she wrote for the *Sunday Graphic* on the Coronation of the young Queen Elizabeth II. Margaret wrote: 'Women can – AND MUST – play a leading part in the creation of a glorious Elizabethan era. Should a woman arise equal to the task, I say let her have an equal chance for the leading Cabinet posts. Why not a woman Chancellor – or Foreign Secretary?' Becoming Prime Minister was beyond her wildest dreams at that point.

Hot on the heels of her Bar studies, she found herself pregnant – expecting twins. Mark and Carol were born by Caesarian section, seven weeks prematurely, in August 1953 at Queen Charlotte's Hospital. They weighed only four pounds each.

Even while awaiting their birth in hospital Margaret concentrated on her career prospects and completed her Bar Finals entrance form. Only four months later she took the exam and began to hunt for chambers. Motherhood was important to Margaret, and in many ways it made her feel complete. She did, however, remark later: 'Of course they become the centre of your life and you live for them as you've never lived for anyone before . . . and yet, I knew that I had something else to give.'

Margaret's career at the bar as a specialist in tax was a fortuitous training. She developed a great facility for mastering complicated briefs quickly which, with a few

At a luncheon reception in London, Mrs Thatcher turned to the photographers and said 'Oh no, they are all plastic – you would think that at a Banker's luncheon for a lady guest they would have real spring flowers, not plastic ones'. 1978.

Top right, Margaret and Denis at Scotney Castle in Kent. *Top left*, Mrs Thatcher calling in at No. 10 in 1978, the year before her election victory. *Bottom right*, With her ginger cat at Scotney Castle. *Bottom left*, Margaret & Denis have a flat in Kent and often spend relaxing weekends there.

deft personal touches, became her own. This ability was to prove invaluable in her later years.

In the meantime Margaret began to hunt seriously for a Parliamentary seat. Because of her career and relatively new motherhood, practical considerations had to come into it – the seat had to be within reach of London. Her hopes rose when she was short-listed for the Orpington by-election. Beckenham, Ashford, Maidstone and others became possibilities but she didn't always reach the short-list. Finally Margaret won the hearts of Finchley, a borough which was considered to be a safe seat. This final breakthrough initiated an inevitable emotional tug of war between Mark and Carol who, at the age of five, were still very young, and her career. Naturally the new seat would require time away from home which was then a spacious and comfortable house near Farnborough, in Kent – and from Finchley it was quite a trek.

And so, at the age of thirty-four, Mrs Margaret Thatcher was duly elected as the Member of Parliament for Finchley. She swept into Westminster looking immaculate, and made a maiden speech that stunned the House. And with a stroke of luck, she was fortunate enough to be balloted to introduce a Private Member's Bill.

By-passing the favoured safe and sensible maiden speech that paid tribute to her constituency, she hurtled into a thirty-minute *tour de force*, arguing for the Public Bodies Bill (admission of the press to meetings) which would allow access to council meetings for the press and public. She spoke fluently and entirely without the benefit of notes on a very complicated piece of legislation – it was a triumph. She was praised for its delivery, described as: 'a speech of front-bench quality', with 'a fluency most of us would envy . . .'.

Within two years she was moved from the back benches and appointed by Prime Minister Harold Macmillan to become Joint Parliamentary Secretary at the Ministry of Pensions – it was her first Government post. She rose admirably to the position and the House was astonished by her first speech at the Dispatch Box, which answered a Labour motion of censure deploring the Government's failure to raise pensions. Margaret, true to form, had done her homework and simply hurtled through reams of figures: the comparative values of pensions over the years; the cost of living in smoking and non-smoking households; the total sums spent on pensions; she was tireless. And as her debating skill grew she rose to the forefront of the party. She sometimes berated the Government, but more often she hit out at the Opposition – whatever her position, the well-aimed attacks and intelligent comments came from a coolly attractive woman whose stature was never shaken by any reaction the House might offer.

When the Conservatives lost the 1964 General Election, Margaret Thatcher moved to the Opposition Front Bench, continuing to shadow at Pensions. A year later, however, when Sir Alec Douglas-Home stood down, Edward Heath took over as leader, he presented Margaret with the wider brief of Housing and Land. Her determination to avoid being side-tracked on 'women's issues' paid off. In 1966, when the Conservatives were again defeated in the General Election, she was given a substantial promotion to Number Two spokesman on Treasury matters under the Shadow Chancellor Iain Macleod. Her years as a tax barrister had been worth while and she found the job and working with Iain Macleod rewarding.

But she had hardly settled when she was back on the move again – and there was only one direction in which to proceed – upwards. And Margaret Thatcher became the Shadow Cabinet spokesman for Fuel and Power. To put it mildly, her rise had been meteoric. Ironically the very man who proposed her for the post, Peter Walker, later served as her Energy Secretary.

Her first day as shadow spokesman was heavy with emotion. The nation wept for the children of the Aberfan disaster – a tragedy that struck when a coal tip fell upon and buried a primary school, killing more than one hundred children and sixteen adults. Margaret, like the rest of the House, was shocked and cannot, to this day, forget the grief that enveloped the tiny village and through that the country. Shortly afterwards, she moved to become Shadow Transport Spokesman.

A major hallmark in her early career came with an invitation to give the lecture at the Conservative Party Conference in Blackpool – a prestigious gesture earmarked only for the high fliers. For Margaret it was her first opportunity to lay down formally her Conservative philosophy. She felt there was too much Government intervention in daily life, suggesting tax incentives to help people to make provision for themselves. Essentially, she felt that there was nothing shameful about people working for larger incomes, and noted that ultimate freedom could be attained by following a life in pursuit of personal achievement. In essence, her philosophy has not, to date, changed.

In 1970, with a wealth of departmental experience in her pocket – she had shadowed five different Governmental departments – she was finally put to the test. Newly-elected Prime Minister Edward Heath appointed her as Secretary of State for Education, a portfolio which she found both challenging and rewarding. Her term was fraught with difficulties, and she inherited an almost impossible brief – her task was to halt the process of making all secondary schools comprehensive. She was bitterly attacked in the House for her refusal to follow the latest tide of education enthusiasm. Naturally education was an issue in which every parent had both a stake and an opinion and she received enormous media attention for her controversial platform. Her role of supporting Heath's promised spending cuts initiated fresh fury – and as expected, her proposals for cuts were greeted with intense condemnation. The necessity of working with the Civil Service – who were not wholly sympathetic to her views – increased the tension and she was, in general, unfavoured by the press and an increasingly dissatisfied nation. Always rather abrasive when under pressure, Margaret was viewed as being over-confident and tough.

Margaret Thatcher finally developed a rapport with the civil servants but it remained on a personal level – for professionally she fought them tooth and nail. Contrary to public perception, her department suffered fewer cuts than any other department save Social Services. This did not, however, rescue her from the complete public roasting she received when she announced that schools would no longer supply free milk for the seven- to eleven-year-olds. Despite the fact that it had already been withdrawn from the secondary-school age group by the previous Labour government, she was labelled 'The Most Unpopular Woman in Britain' by *Sun* editorial staff while cries of 'Thatcher, Thatcher, Milk Snatcher' echoed above her head.

And matters did not improve as she attempted to stem the flow of funds into the National Union of Students – funds that financed activities that were completely unrelated to student welfare. Because the money was being spent on political issues that did not always affect Britain, she felt it was a natural area in which to make cuts. The ensuing uproar brought her as close as she has ever been to bending under stress. By Christmas 1970, some whispered that she might resign and an anxious Denis Thatcher suggested she 'Chuck it in'. The abuse was violent – demonstrations greeted her everywhere, particularly at the universities. At Liverpool paper darts were hurled down on her and students became so disorderly that she had to be led out by a side door. As Penny Junor notes in her book *Margaret Thatcher*, she later confessed, 'It was

Margaret and Denis Thatcher at their home in Flood Street.

a very rowdy meeting,' and opened her blouse to a close friend revealing an enormous bruise on her chest. Someone had hit her with a stone egg. 'It did hurt like mad,' she said. 'Give me a nice hot cup of tea. I have still two more speaking engagements this afternoon.'

Her years on the Education front may not have been her happiest but they reinforced to her the importance of an iron will and steely nerve under pressure. It also taught her that personal popularity may be helpful but is not essential to pressing through policies. It was a pity that her real achievements were buried under the welter of criticism. For it is not often remembered that it was Margaret Thatcher who channelled funds to rebuild primary schools; attempted to raise the school leaving age; and most importantly, refused even to consider abolishing the Open University.

Until then Margaret Thatcher had been a highly competent departmental leader – perhaps no great orator or favourite in the House, but strong and steady under pressure and willing to fight for what she believed in. A formidable opponent and a tough colleague she was a puzzle to her contemporaries and she found herself with a low ranking around the Cabinet table. Future leader was not a role anyone would have expected her to play; however, behind the scenes events were beginning to move.

In February 1974 Edward Heath lost the General Election, and with the Conservatives again in opposition, Margaret Thatcher took over as Shadow Minister of the Environment. It was a vast and complex brief, with a frightening work load. She did, however, shoulder the lot and in her capacity found herself speaking more frequently than any of her colleagues. The exposure did not do her any harm.

In the meantime the Party had become disenchanted with Ted Heath's leadership – it was time for a change. Already Sir Keith Joseph, an old friend and ally of Margaret Thatcher's, had formed an informal think-tank for realigning the entire Conservative philosophy. Sir Keith persuaded Edward Heath to support setting up a research body – the purpose of which he described to Penny Junor in *Margaret Thatcher*:

'I realized that we had allowed our good intentions to run away with us, and I was anxious to try to learn the lessons of what had happened, and in particular why the Germans had done so well with their social market philosophy. . . . When Mr Heath offered me a position in his Shadow Cabinet, I asked him to let me have a place without portfolio so that I could set up a little research body to find out the lessons from Western Europe, and to find out why their prosperity was so much better than ours.'

Thus the Centre of Policy Studies was born, but as it transpired, the Centre fell under the guidance of director Alfred Sherman, a journalist and ex-Communist whose total commitment then leant towards monetarism. The Centre was therefore rather more focused on applying the lessons of social market thinking to Britain. Alfred, small and bull-like, was to have an important influence on Margaret Thatcher in later years, and this allegiance was a turning point in Conservatism. The move away from Government control, decentralization; the proposal to let market forces find their own level; and the initiation of tax incentives to revive the benumbed economy were only some of the ideology he represented. Margaret Thatcher was no blind follower to the thinking. She came to it by instinct.

Inflation, which is caused by too much money in circulation, can be curbed in a number of ways. The monetarists, who strayed from the traditional theory of curbing it at source, claimed that unemployment should be allowed to rise as the Government gets to grips with inflation, to allow for new economic industries to rise out of the ashes and take the labour in to more productive fields. It was a brave stance, but heresy to many – particularly the traditional 'wets' of the Conservative Party. While these proposed policies were being tossed around among party members, moves were being made to replace Edward Heath – the Conservative Party decided that he was no longer an asset.

The leadership struggle that ensued was fascinating, for Margaret Thatcher was not listed as a contender until the very end of the campaign. Potential candidates came and went as Edward du Cann, Willie Whitelaw and Sir Keith Joseph vied for power – for different reasons each fell by the wayside. There was a yawning gap to be filled. Colditz Hero, Airey Neave, was one man who spotted Margaret Thatcher as a future leader. He first met Margaret while studying for the Bar, and his optimism and support were vital to her campaign. He was an unlikely ally for socially they were very different – from a comfortable, male-orientated and middle-class background, he was very much Establishment; a class that Margaret Thatcher, the grocer's daughter from Grantham, had never learned to mix easily with.

Until Keith Joseph withdrew from the race Margaret Thatcher did not run and it was alone that she decided to put herself forward. In simple terms, she saw it as a means to rescue the Conservative Party and clearly re-establish their philosophy to the right. She felt that it was time to stand up for individual respect and with her imagination, clear-headedness and political instinct she developed a manageable philosophy that would have a resounding impact.

Sharing the common aim to defeat Edward Heath in the leadership ballot, Thatcher and Neave worked well together and with a tiny campaign of barely half a dozen activists who met in huddles in Margaret Thatcher's office – they were small fish in comparison with Edward Heath's massive heavy-weight team. Their advantage, however, was sheer determination and commitment – they *had* to win. Airey Neave and his team put in hours and hours of quiet lobbying, taking aside back-bench MPs, asking for their views and gently suggesting the name Thatcher; nary a stone was left unturned. By a stroke of good fortune Edward Heath had – perhaps to his own detriment – appointed Margaret to the front bench to become the Second Shadow Treasury spokesman supporting Robert Carr. She prepared powerful and opinionated speeches, attacking the Labour Government and clearly setting her platform as potential leader. The Finance Bill debate clearly illustrated her remarkable abilities and she dominated the House – taking her to the forefront of the Conservative ranks.

With Gordon Reece's help she wooed a sceptical Fleet Street, spelling out her ideas to set Britain back on its feet. Her platform was replete with hard facts and with her plain, direct manner of speech and her pretty and clearly feminine appearance, she was a disconcerting figure.

The day for the first ballot dawned and on the surface the polls looked gloomy. Few, however, had reckoned with the badger-like work of Airey Neave – he'd been here, there and *everywhere*. The results of his dedication and persistence were astounding – Margaret Thatcher beat Edward Heath by a vote of 130 to 119. Ted Heath, who had been ultimately confident, was shocked to the core: 'So,' he said tersely, 'we got it all wrong.'

A second ballot came one very long week later. Astonished by the success of the first ballot, the Thatcher household in Flood Street, Chelsea, could scarcely breathe. And when the result of the second one came, they were flabbergasted. Airey Neave walked into his office at the House where Margaret, consumed with nerves, was

Top right, Margaret Thatcher is hoisted at an Earl's Court Exhibition in 1978. Top left, In Brighton, 1978, Margaret is showered with birthday cards. Bottom, Blackpool Conservative Party Conference in 1978, the crowd applaud the new Party leader Mrs Margaret Thatcher.

waiting. He said simply, 'It's all right. You're the Leader of the Opposition.'

Following a short but highly charged celebration, she immediately set to work. Margaret Thatcher's initial task was to write some notes for her first press conference as leader. The Grand Committee Room on the ground floor off Westminster Hall was packed as she entered and proudly said, 'To me it is like a dream, that the next name on the list after Harold Macmillan, Sir Alex Douglas-Home and Edward Heath is Margaret Thatcher. . .'.

The next four years which constituted the run-up to the 1979 General Election were not easy for the new leader. For a start, she had to establish herself within the

31

Conservative Party which was still reeling slightly from the shock of being led by a woman. The breakthrough rally took place at the Conservative Party Conference that year in Blackpool; and her first speech to the faithful was a vital one – she had to win their hearts. Countless days and nights were spent on the preparation of her speech. And playwright Ronald Millar and his team worked straight through the night before the Conference writing and rewriting the text. Ronnie Millar remembers her dissatisfaction with every attempt and her dogged determination to get it right: 'No, no,' said Margaret over and over again. 'That's not me. We must try again.' She didn't sleep that night; but on Friday, driven by adrenalin and nerves, and immaculately dressed, she appeared before the expectant crowd. She broke the tension on the rostrum by mopping the lectern with a blue feather duster handed to her by a party worker. The audience loved it and from then on she could do no wrong – it was a triumph.

Welding together a Shadow Cabinet was less easy. Margaret had basically inherited Edward Heath's team and they never really did catch on to her enthusiasm and ideas for restructuring Britain. Her one big support was Willie Whitelaw. Shrewd, avuncular, and a figure of enormous Conservative Party respect, he was just the man to give her the shoulder she needed – although it did take him some time to genuinely stand behind her. She brought Sir Keith Joseph into her ranks in a roving policy and research capacity and he kept up his close links with the Centre for Policy Studies – discreetly pushing Conservative thinking back to the right, much to the discomfiture of his colleagues and, in particular, Jim Prior. Thatcher's teething problems were insignificant, however, when compared with the state of the British economy. With the Labour Government stumbling from disaster to disaster, inflation was rampant and prices soared everywhere. The nation's debt was running at an all-time high and high public spending was rampant. The situation was uncontrollable. Overseas countries referred to the 'British Disease' when Britain was forced to apply for a massive loan from the International Monetary Fund.

Strikes had literally brought Britain's productivity to a standstill and the 1978 'Winter of Discontent' stamped the final seal of desolation on a country that had once been a world leader. And as discussed earlier, Prime Minister Callaghan returned from a meeting in sunny Guadeloupe feigning virtual ignorance of the British plight.

It was as if the country had tumbled into a dreadful nightmare as the chaos of the trade union movement broke loose. Lorry and tanker drivers pulled off the road, demanding immediate 25 per cent wage rises. Picketers stood outside the hospitals blocking admissions – stonily facing the pleas of patients who were seeking treatment. Ambulance men and women refused to transport the sick and injured, and cemetery workers did not bury the dead – piling them up in the morgues because of the picket action. Dockyards were stacked with deteriorating food due to the transportation strike, and violent fighting broke out amongst the picketers. The Underground system ceased to run; refuse collectors left the rubbish piling up in the streets; a strike of school caretakers kept half a million children at home; while other public servants running the water and sewage systems went out. Television recorded these events for the world to view and as Britain crawled her way through a miserably cold winter, patriotism died. One hospital official actually admitted, 'If people die, so be it.'

Top, **R**emembrance Day, 1987. Prime Minister Margaret Thatcher carries a poppy wreath as David Owen, James Molyneaux, David Steele and Neil Kinnock look on. *Bottom*, Margaret Thatcher greets constituency members during her 1979 Election campaign.

Opposite, **R**elaxing with a book in her Downing Street sitting room, 1988. *Top*, Margaret Thatcher clutches a bouquet of freshly picked spring flowers as she relaxes at the Thatcher weekend home in Kent. *Bottom*, Margaret and Denis enjoy the Kent countryside on one of their weekend jaunts.

Top, **P**rime Minister Margaret Thatcher addresses her guests at a Downing Street reception. *Bottom*, Margaret Thatcher finalizes arrangements from the Campaign bus during the 1983 Election.

Top, **P**atriotism reaches a new high as the Falklands ships sail into Portsmouth – tears of joy fill the eyes of the flag-waving crowds. *Bottom*, Margaret Thatcher leaves a local church service in 1982.

Opposite, **M**rs Margaret Thatcher and Premier Mikhail Gorbachev forming a close relationship – an indication of the changing international affairs. *Top*, Sojourns in the countryside have always been a favourite past-time for Margaret and Denis Thatcher. *Bottom*, Hard at work in her study at No. 10 Downing Street.

Top, **P**arty confidence soars at the Conservative Party Conference in Blackpool, 1987. *Bottom*, Flowers from Denis? Margaret Thatcher greets photographers from the back of her car.

The country was tired and dispirited and Margaret Thatcher felt that it was time to take control. The previous years had built her confidence and experience – the time had come: the Government had to fall. In March of 1979 James Callaghan lost a vote of confidence in the House, following the collapse of the Government's devolution policy. On that night, the tellers' announcement that the Labour Government had fallen by one vote brought a tremendous response – the pent-up emotion of the preceding months, and even years, exploded. As Margaret Thatcher sat in her place on the front bench of the Opposition, Willie Whitelaw instinctively put his arm round her. It was her chance – it was finally her turn. The Conservatives cheered; the Labour Party looked grim and dismayed – the race was on.

Blackpool, 1976. Margaret Thatcher wears her famous 'beehive' hat.

CHAPTER THREE
THE RACE FOR DOWNING STREET

Elation lifted the hearts of the Conservatives and the nation as a whole. The seeds of change were sown and the country waited in anticipation. The campaign strategy had been planned and ready for months and needed only to be put into action. One of the key architects was Airey Neave. The campaign took an almost scientific approach – carefully analysing potential support groups among the newly-turned Conservative working classes. British society had become more mobile and it was the new Conservatives who had the strongest feelings about the increasing lawlessness in the country. Margaret's clear-cut vision of law and order appealed. She targeted women in council homes, Labour households, and the skilled manual workers who had ambitions for a better future. The nation cried out for more freedom; the chance to own their own homes; improved education; a control of the cost of living – it was Margaret Thatcher's philosophy and it appealed to them. She offered choice, and, above all, could release them from the shackles of a mismanaged government.

It almost became a social revolution – Britain was on the verge of a change which would set the pattern for decades to come. Perhaps few people consciously chose Margaret Thatcher – it may well have been an instinctive swing of party allegiances brought about by intense dissatisfaction that changed Britain's vote. In those early days, many wondered just how long she would hold on to power before she would be ousted by the loss of an election or by her own party.

Always quietly behind her was Airey Neave. In some ways they might have seemed an odd couple, but their uniting force was his enormous respect for her ability, and her admiration for his war-time record. He had the foresight to appreciate her greatest asset, saying of her, 'Margaret is the first real idealist politician for a long time. She is a philospher as well as politician.' He became her Svengali, Kingmaker almost. There was a magnetic pull which drew them to each other. Being older, he could talk to her in a frank way that others could not. He also knew how to handle her as a woman. Margaret, after all, was and is intensely feminine. Other senior politicians who have won a special working relationship understanding this element were Lord Carrington, Humphrey Atkins and Cecil Parkinson.

The pre-election excitement and enthusiasm lasted only two days into her campaign. Airey Neave was blown up by the IRA in his car as he drove out of the

The Young Conservatives present Margaret Thatcher with a Valentine's Day card.

House of Commons car park. At the time, Margaret Thatcher had been making her rounds in Finchley.

The message that a bomb had gone off in the House of Commons had been phoned through to her but she was told no further details. Derek Howe, then her press secretary, broke the news. 'Please God, don't let it be Airey' was reported to be her initial reaction.

She nonetheless carried out her scheduled engagements with a visit to the BBC for a party political broadcast. Derek Howe received the confirmation that it was Airey Neave who had been hit. He went straight to the BBC to tell Margaret the news. 'I have bad news,' he said quietly, 'they have Airey.' Her shock was visible. With characteristic calm, Margaret Thatcher swallowed her grief and, gathering all her emotional resources, she cancelled the broadcast, and drove immediately to the House.

'You could sense the blow,' said Derek Howe later. 'He was so special to her. She went very silent.' The shock was indeed colossal, made worse perhaps because of the fact that she had given Airey Neave the position of Shadow Secretary for Northern Ireland – her choice had cost him his life. Arriving in her office she went straight to her desk and within twenty minutes had written a tribute into which she poured the emotion that her highly-guarded composure forbade:

'The assassination of Airey Neave has left his friends and colleagues as stunned and grief-stricken as his family. He was one of freedom's warriors. Courageous, staunch, true, he lived for his beliefs and now he has died for them. A gentle, brave and unassuming man, he was a loyal and very dear friend. He had a wonderful family who supported him in everything he did. Now there is a gap in our lives which cannot be filled.'

The last statement held more truth than she could have ever imagined. Throughout the ensuing campaign and following years she was often heard to sigh, 'How I miss Airey'. The funeral took place one week later.

Highly concerned about the well-being of Neave's widow, Diana, Margaret encouraged her to join in the election campaign in an attempt to distract her from her enveloping grief. Giving Diana Neave a new purpose did help her through the first stages of grief and together they worked for the victory that would have pleased Neave so deeply. Margaret later ennobled her as Baroness Airey of Abingdon where she took her seat in the House of Lords as a tribute to her husband.

While Airey was the architect of policy and strategy, cigar-smoking Gordon Reece was responsible for the public image of Margaret Thatcher and in turn he secured Saatchi and Saatchi. The advertising agency, headed by the dynamic Saatchi brothers, worked with their whiz-kid managing director Tim Bell, to create the most effective, hard-hitting and emotionally charged campaign the Conservative Party had ever witnessed.

But Gordon Reece had ideas of his own for Margaret. His first challenge was to find a way of modulating her voice when forced to make herself heard above a baying

House of Commons or public meeting. A woman's voice becomes shrill when raised and hers was no exception. They sought advice from Ronnie Millar, who as a playwright was quite familiar with techniques to acquire a good theatrical voice. 'Try humming,' he said, sending a female voice trainer to help. He advised lowering the voice, which in turn slowed the speed of speech – 'Stick to that when under pressure in the House. The voice will then drive through the hubbub.'

Gordon Reece suggested that she simplify her hairstyles for television, and wear simple, clean-cut clothing with a minimum of jewellery. Television was always Margaret Thatcher's pet peeve. She has never felt happy or comfortable with that medium and even today, with her years of experience, she would prefer to avoid such appearances.

The decision of which television interviews to accept was left to Gordon, and with his eye on the new electorate – very often female – he chose soft, mid-morning shows like Jimmy Young, Jimmy Savile and Gerald Harper; and during the campaign he arranged a slot for her on Radio 4's 'Election Call'. Perhaps most importantly, however, he ensured Margaret managed one newsworthy activity every day, in time to be shown in the early evening national news bulletins, which were targeted at families who would often be together over their evening meal. Political television interviewers were carefully screened: hostile left-wing sympathies would only bring out Thatcher's often harshly competitive instinct.

The early courtship of newspaper editors paid off, particularly with the daily populars like the *Sun, Daily Mail* and *Daily Express* who were generous in their coverage.

The exhaustive daily routine was shattering for the team, save Margaret Thatcher herself. Her daughter Carol returned from work in Australia to lend moral support while Denis loyally stood alongside her on every engagement.

Her message was simple enough – as the Conservative manifesto boomed: 'This election is about the future of Britain – a great country which seems to have lost its way.' And to guarantee that everyone got the message, Margaret set an unparalleled pace. She left home at the crack of dawn each day, suitcase already carefully packed the night before with tissue paper and changes of clothing. She did her own make-up unless there was a television appearance and her own hair with the help of her heated hair rollers – organization was the key to her whole operation and its sheer speed was virtually electric. With speedy changes made en route and even faster changes to rewritten speeches, it was not unknown for husband Denis to be seen furiously sticking together bits of the next speech with Sellotape.

They rarely returned before 2 a.m. and although supper would already be cooked, Margaret relaxed by becoming the housewife and hostess again – busily laying the table and fussing over her working team. Out on the road she was in her element. She loved meeting people and holding spontaneous conversations – she developed the marvellous ability to concentrate on one conversation as the meetings were disrupted and often drowned out by hordes of press photographers angling for better shots.

In the streets and on the rostrum set speeches became a thing of the past. Confident in her message, and indeed her mission, her addresses took on a fresh spontaneity and zeal. Her passion was unmistakable – the electorate loved it. And

Top right, Newly elected Leader of the Conservative Party, Margaret Thatcher, meets the Press in the House of Commons Committee Room. *Bottom right*, Margaret and Denis Thatcher in flight for a tour of Britain during the 1979 General Election campaign. *Top*, Trade Union support for the Conservatives, 1979. *Bottom*, Margaret Thatcher canvassing in an election walkabout.

DATE	NAME	ADDRESS
ul /79	*Margaret Thatcher*	*In transit – hoping to move.*

Top In East Anglia, two days before the General Election, Margaret Thatcher made this entry in a guest book. *Bottom*, The famous Saatchi & Saatchi poster of the unemployed, 1978. *Opposite*, Wembley Mass Trade Unions Rally for the Conservative Party members in 1979.

Margaret Thatcher in turn blossomed and became radiant; some said brighter and prettier by the moment.

She urged the public on – it was time for Britain to catch up with the free world: 'It is time we became a leader, not a straggler. Unless we change our ways and our direction, our greatness as a nation will soon be a footnote in the history books. . .'. Photographs of that period were memorable. Always portrayed in unique circumstance, the most comic was perhaps in Ely, Suffolk, where she awkwardly posed for fifteen minutes with a day-old calf. Concerned for the well-being of the animal, Denis worriedly cautioned her: 'You're going to have a half-dead calf on your hands in a minute.' And the action never ceased. She was photographed using a sewing machine, sweeping a floor and gaily touring a chocolate factory. With her remarkable capacity to accommodate, she clearly enjoyed her experiences; and photographs presented her as a simple, caring woman – an image that served as a foil to her serious and hard-headed political persona.

Meanwhile Prime Minister James Callaghan had mounted a formidable campaign. Lacking the lustre of the Thatcher campaign, it nonetheless carried a heavy-weight message – 'Steady as you go with a leave-it-to-me'. It was a slogan that paid tribute to his international standing and experience. He was portrayed as a knowledgeable and comforting national figurehead who often illuminated Margaret's inexperience and, sometimes patent, insecurity. Although there was no personal antagonism between Callaghan and Margaret Thatcher, he could not bring himself to refer to her by name – choosing instead to refer to her only as 'the Leader of the Conservative Party'. Polls, however, were not always encouraging for Margaret. Her personal rating was never high, partly because of reservations held by the electorate regarding a woman Prime Minister. She lagged behind Callaghan throughout the campaign. Margaret Thatcher's policies were, however, popular and scored well in the opinion polls. The Conservatives did lead throughout the campaign but the polls shifted dramatically as the Conservatives dropped from their pinnacle of an 11 per cent majority to only 5 per cent in the final days.

Overall the campaign was conducted in high spirits, and with the positive goals and commitment of the Conservative Party, Britain could not have chosen better. Margaret Thatcher could not have failed – she had been waiting too long and she was more than ready. The rehearsal was over.

CHAPTER FOUR
A DAY IN THE LIFE

Number 10 Downing Street is largely a gracious office with state rooms and private residence combined; it was once described as a 'gentleman's home in which a little government takes place from time to time'. Today the role has been reversed. Now there are over 130 people beavering away and according to their status are working in offices of varying grandeur; although none of the offices, bar that of the Prime Minister, is very splendid. The traditional English view that it is somehow unsuitable for the heads of government to be seen working in great splendour precludes luxury. The offices at No. 10 Downing Street invariably compare badly with Prime Ministers' offices and residences internationally.

Number 10 does, however, score on one point – it retains a certain home-spun charm with the comfort of a discreet country house. The policeman at the front door congenially greets – by name – all who enter. Tucked away in his little side room is the ubiquitous kettle simmering with the Englishman's brew – tea.

Upstairs, on the first floor, overlooking the gardens is the Prime Minister's room. Far from being ostentatious, it attains a very English-style elegance with discreet, pale cream walls; good brocade curtains; four comfortable chairs arranged around a table at one end, with a yellow winged chair for Mrs Thatcher; and at the other end of the spacious room, spanning three windows, Margaret Thatcher's desk. Clearly an organized and efficient worker, Margaret Thatcher keeps her commodious desk virtually free of clutter. A small vase of flowers sits prettily on the large desk – a feminine touch that defies the masculine proportions of the desk. The walls are hung with a discreet collection of fine paintings.

A visit to the Prime Minister follows a routine. Visitors wait in a small and tastefully furnished room on the ground floor, with copies of *The Economist* and daily papers for entertainment, until invited upstairs by the Political Private Secretary. The famous staircase is flanked by photographs of past premiers – James Callaghan's colour portrait appearing slightly incongruous next to the otherwise monotone photos – and on the booklined landing is an attractive octagonal table. Mrs Thatcher energetically strides to the door; she is informal, but clearly and charismatically in charge. Bidding in and seating the visitors she sits down in her favourite wing arm chair. Margaret Thatcher has always felt more comfortable sitting upright and even during the most gruelling of meetings, she does not slouch – another indication of the immense self-control she encompasses.

After half an hour, she presses a bell for coffee and it is brought in on a large, oval tray, laden with white, gold-rimmed bone china cups, a solid English silver tea pot, a silver jug and sugar bowl. Perhaps somewhat surprising the Prime Minister

Top right, **T**he 'char' at number 10. Margaret Thatcher found it unsuitable for another woman to be washing her step and upon arriving at Downing Street, she released the chars from this task. *Top left,* The morning delivery at No 10. *Bottom,* Margaret Thatcher relaxes in her study after a day's work.

Mrs Thatcher supervising the arrangements for a dinner in honour of Her Majesty The Queen Mother.

serves instant coffee and she makes no apology for it. 'So much more convenient,' she explains, discussing the virtues of one brand against another. Convenience is an important element of life at No. 10, for there is no resident housekeeper nor, indeed, staff available to provide silver service. The coffee was kindly made up and presented by the security staff.

Any personal service that Mrs Thatcher might require is competently taken care of by her private personal secretary, Joy Robillard. Once secretary to Airey Neave, she has no objection to dashing out for groceries or personal supplies. Unlike Chequers, the Prime Ministerial country home in Buckinghamshire where a full-time housekeeper, Miss Thomas is retained, everything in London is done on an ad hoc basis. Upstairs, in her private flat, Margaret cooks for herself or with the assistance of Joy. Visitors are often nonplussed by the sight of their Prime Minister rummaging in the freezer for ice and drinks. On one occasion she invited her Parliamentary Private Secretary, Ian Gow, and Tory MP George Gardiner back to Downing Street for supper. The two men sat in wonder, awkwardly watching the news on TV, as she ferreted through cupboards – 'You must be hungry; let me get you something,' she said briskly. Preparing Chicken Kiev, frozen peas and some other vegetables, she efficiently served the startled men – who were disconcerted by her domesticity.

During his term of office James Callaghan instigated the motion that the Prime Minister must pay 10 per cent of his (or her) salary for the privilege of living at No. 10. In addition the Prime Minister must pay all the running costs of the main part of the house; the wages and salaries of domestic staff and all personal entertaining. Government entertaining for banquets is footed by the state. Thatcher's first state banquet for German Chancellor Helmut Schmidt got off to a rocky start. The Prime Minister was appalled to discover that No. 10 had no silver cutlery for entertaining heads of state – and she had no qualms about letting her feelings be known. Quick to react, Marcus Kimball, MP for the Gainsborough division of Lincolnshire, gallantly approached a fellow Lincolnshire Tory, Lord Brownlow, who owns the magnificent Belton House. Brownlow generously complied and a loan of family silver, in sufficient quantity and quality to suit a state banquet, was ferried carefully to London.

Economy has always been a foremost consideration of Margaret. On the day she became Prime Minister she discovered there was nothing to put together a meal at No. 10, and undaunted, she arranged for a chicken casserole from her own freezer at Flood Street to be brought over. And when it comes to flowers – she always has strict instructions for her florist – 'Don't waste a flower. Trim back the stalks and keep the displays going right to the end!' she will direct. Prudently, she even went as far as to purchase a good supply of everlasting Christmas decorations. Her displays are more expansive today than in the early days and the front hall displays are glorious arrangements.

Margaret Thatcher regards Downing Street very much as her home, and takes much pride in entertaining guests personally. Indeed, she and Denis always appear to be enjoying themselves during the social occasions they host, making sure their guests have a good time. Every detail is supervised by herself, right down to the catering details of the canapés they serve at the receptions. On these occasions she throws open the first-floor reception rooms at the back of the house, overlooking Horse Guards Parade. The interlinked state rooms – with their blue and white damask walls they are perfect backdrops for the magnificent Old Masters that line them. Her particularly favourite painting 'Men with Horses Crossing a River' hangs over the fireplace in one room. Three Turners were brought in from the British Embassy in Paris and, as a personal touch, Mrs Thatcher insisted on original portraits of Nelson and Wellington to complete the décor. Mrs Thatcher's personal interests are illustrated by the busts of Britain's foremost scientists – Joseph Priestley who discovered oxygen; Sir Humphry Davy, the inventor of the miner's lamp; and Michael Faraday who founded the theory of electro-magnetics.

Margaret Thatcher's day begins at 6.30 a.m.; a habit she developed early in life. She finds four to five hours' sleep is quite sufficient although she does sleep an hour or two later at weekends. Upon awakening she immediately switches on Radio 4 and the *Today* programme – occasionally even catching some of *Farming Today* which precedes it. Invariably, she cooks a proper breakfast for Denis – it is a ritual that has taken place since the beginning of her marriage. So important is it, that once during her term as Secretary of State for Education she broke off discussions on the multi-million-pound budget to put on her hat and coat and rush off to buy Denis's bacon before closing time. On returning, she slipped off her coat, sank down at her desk and asked the astonished civil servants, 'Now where were we? . . .' Her figure indicates her own breakfast habits: she has a cup of coffee, a glass of orange juice and a Vitamin C tablet. At weekends she unwinds a little, however, and allows the housekeeper to prepare some toast and marmalade.

The official working day begins at 8.30 a.m. Reading the newspaper is a perfunctory exercise, but surprisingly she does not read them from cover to cover. Instead they are predigested for her, with irrelevant gossip left out. Articles of political and topical interest are filed. Perhaps understandably, she doesn't choose to read either biographical articles about herself or any personal commentary of a hurtful or insulting nature.

At 8.30 she goes over the daily programme with her personal staff in her study. Then the round of meetings begins: the Cabinet meet at least once a week for two hours. In her early years as Prime Minister, she found these meetings unnecessarily tense – her Cabinet were not wholly supportive of her Thatcherite philosophy and she found that she would rather get on with the job than present continual justifications for her theories. Twice a week – on Tuesdays and Thursdays – she is obliged to answer questions at the Dispatch Box in the House of Commons. This particular responsibility requires much preparation and rehearsal – experts are called in; and examples of almost every possible question that can be hurled at her across the floor are carefully considered. Question Time in the House is a uniquely British institution and an excellent example of democracy at its answerable best. The Prime Minister can never be allowed to duck questions from her electorate or Parliament. Her answers are beamed across the nation by radio. It has to be a faultless performance – and so it is.

Tuesdays are most notable for her regular audience with the Queen at Buckingham Palace. It is a pity that, over the years, sniggering has emerged from royal circles at the almost glutinous respect Margaret Thatcher has always held for her monarch. Because the Prime Minister is not easily relaxed and has always highly regarded the monarchical institution, her rather formal approaches have often been deemed obsequious. Her predecessors James Callaghan and Harold Wilson had naturally chatty personalities which endeared them to the Queen.

Informal relations between No. 10 Downing Street and Buckingham Palace have been occasionally strained particularly when a member of the Royal Family is thought to have criticized the government of the day in any manner. Feelings ran high over remarks made about the Conservative Government record on the inner city – and were later rectified.

Feelings were ruffled at an early stage in Margaret Thatcher's premiership when a debate arose about whether it was safe for the Queen to attend the Lusaka Commonwealth Conference. Downing Street's message was 'I will decide if it is safe'. But by return came the reply, 'I am going. I am head of the Commonwealth and nothing will stop me.' Both very dedicated women with a mission to fulfil, it is inevitable that they would occasionally clash; particularly since cowardice is in neither's nature.

On another occasion it was Prince Philip who vocalized frustration with his Prime Minister. It was Margaret Thatcher's decision that Britain would not participate in

Top right, Mrs Thatcher prepares the tea at her home in Flood Street. *Top left*, In her study at Downing Street, 1982.
Bottom, Downing Street, 1984

the Moscow Olympic Games, to protest against the invasion of Afghanistan. Prince Philip, dedicated to his role as President of the International Equestrian Federation, objected. 'I should go,' he said, 'I have a duty to go . . . Politicians are trying to control us. If only they would accept that politics and sport do not mix.'

Conceivably, the Royal Family see themselves as the conscience of the nation in rather the same way that the established church does. Certainly feelings were bruised when the Queen's Press Secretary, Michael Shea, unofficially admitted that the Queen was deeply concerned about the biting effects of the Prime Minister's first phase in turning the economy around. Admittedly, unemployment was running high before the more prosperous results of Thatcherism became evident. The criticism hurt Margaret Thatcher, for it would never have occurred to her to comment on the Queen and she has not done so. Her audiences are extremely private, and not a word is ever passed on.

Family time, whether it be in the attic flat upstairs, or at Chequers, has always been brief but affectionate. Early on in their married life, Margaret and Denis decided that their work would come first; and they would fit their family in and around it. That is not, under any circumstances, to say they did not care for Carol and Mark; they did and do deeply. It was more a question of personal style in their management of the family home. Quality rather than quantity of time is most important. Although it can be said that Margaret was never a cosy person, perhaps most comfortable and energized with trails of people coming in for tea parties and general socializing, she has always acknowledged how much strength she has derived from the family unit. And as they in turn have endlessly demonstrated, they are there to back her up on any occasion great or small – General Election campaigns, overseas tours or simply dinners at No. 10.

Daughter Carol, now twenty-seven, has an instinct for when to telephone 'Mum'. Any crisis and Carol is on the line – it is a relationship that has developed almost sisterly connotations. Throughout each election campaign she becomes her mother's personal manager, organizing everything from clothes and messages to hair rollers. In a crisis they have occasionally even swopped clothes. Certainly Carol's account of her mother's General Election campaign in *Diary of an Election*, 1983 was full of humorous entries like 'Help, however am I going to manage Mum's extensive wardrobe?' as she surveyed rails of outfits, each perfectly matched with shoes in their categories, that ranged from 'executive suits' to 'clodhopper' shoes for walkabouts. She has shoes for speech making (they must be comfortable when standing), clothes that can stand up to missiles of flour, eggs or tomatoes, and particular clothing for television and evening events. At the end of the campaign, victory secure, and safely back in her bedroom at Downing Street, Carol said 'Congratulations, I am thrilled for you. It's history.' And as her Mum, the newly elected Prime Minister climbed into bed, she reflected, 'But history, when you're making it, doesn't seem like history. They expect you to jump up and down but you're always thinking of the next job in hand. . . .' And from that summation her next thought was, 'I wonder if there is world news', and she picked up the bedside transistor radio. It was 5 a.m.!

Carol, who was academically successful at school and who earned her spurs as a thoroughly professional journalist, does not resemble her mother in appearance, being taller and heavier in build. She has a bright, breezy personality, and cares little for formality – never seeking the limelight or taking a stand on any ceremony. As a child she was cheerful and relaxed – no doubt curious about what life would have been like if her mother had been like others. There were times, naturally, when Carol resented the 'Red Box' which would distract her mother just as she wanted to tell her something. Overall, however, it was and is a happy and harmonious relationship.

Her son Mark is equally treasured. Mark is handsome, a good sportsman – if somewhat less academically inclined than Carol – and he is a successful entrepreneur. He sometimes has been criticized for sailing too near the wind and trading too much on his mother's name. Although he never sought a professional career, which contradicts to a certain degree the upbringings of his parents, he is certainly a fine example of Thatcher policy in that he found his niche in the entrepreneurial world. Unlike Carol, he did not choose university, branching off immediately into his own style of business. Today, married and living in Texas, he has amassed a considerable fortune.

Mark did not inherit his mother's intellectual brilliance nor does he exude his father's easy-going charm – it was his pomposity that became evident in his schooldays. Despite their differences, the bond between mother and son is very strong indeed. For a woman who can very often appear to be a rather harsh and determined figure when it comes to policy making, she could be described as being soft and vulnerable emotionally with regard to her family. Friends and colleagues will always remember the day she almost collapsed when the news came through that Mark, taking part in the Paris to Dakar car rally, had gone missing in the Sahara Desert. It was a tremendously upsetting time for Margaret who broke down in public and had enormous difficulty concentrating on any business at hand. Prime-ministerial duties were virtually forgotten as she became first and foremost a mother. There have been very few completely and utterly low spots in her career – this was one of them. She was sick with worry, imagining the very worst, and allowing press reports of people who had perished in the harsh desert to haunt her.

She managed to get through a morning Cabinet meeting upon hearing the news, but was completely caught off guard when a pressman later asked if there was any news. 'I'm sorry, there is no news,' she said, tears welling up. 'Naturally I am very concerned,' and unable to control the emotion, she sobbed desperately for a few moments. Somehow, her strength returned and she managed to turn to the matter in hand and deliver a twenty-five-minute, after-lunch speech but she was visibly shaken.

The foundation of Margaret Thatcher's life is her relationship with her husband Denis. He has been the support upon which her entire career has been built. It would be fair to say that while their marriage has never been described as being passionately romantic, it is solid and they are both firmly entrenched in it – undeniably very happy and close. Denis not only brought Margaret financial security, a luxury she has always paid tribute to, but he has also brought her undying loyalty and friendship. He totally understands her needs and she confides in him as she does in no one else. She has fiercely defended criticism of her wearing a string of pearls saying in an uncharacteristic

Top right, Carol Thatcher, trout fishing. *Top left,* Mark Thatcher, following his first racing win. *Bottom,* The Thatcher family at Chequers, 1981. *Opposite,* Christmas, 1981.

Top right, Margaret gives Denis a helping hand after his morning golf practice at Chequers. *Top left,* A kiss from Denis following her return from a visit to the Far East. *Bottom,* An attentive Denis at the Conservative Party Conference in Brighton.

outburst, 'I will bloody well wear them. They were given to me by Denis.' Her speech writer Sir Ronald Millar riposted, 'If only you would speak like that on television. They would love you for it!'

The *Private Eye* skit on Denis in the 'Dear Bill' letters may have touched on apsects of his personality, but it would not be fair to write him off as the gin-drinking Englishman despite the fact that he does quite often say, 'Just time for a tincture', has some volatile views on the 'bolshies' who run the trade unions and the 'pinkoes' who run the BBC.

Indeed, he has never been afraid to give leash to his feelings, occasionally to the excruciating embarrassment of his wife's aides. During the period that the high-profile activities of the Greenham Common anti-nuclear protesters were getting press attention he commented, 'Ah, roubles from Moscow, roubles from Moscow.' He is clearly loved, by those who know him, for his down-to-earth self-righteousness. He's not perfect and he does swear, much to Margaret's dismay. As he arrived late for the Oxford and Cambridge Boat Race one year, he scrambled aboard the accompanying launch and donning a jockey cap calmly stated, 'The fucking driver got lost!'

Behind the congenial host of Downing Street receptions and banquets lies a man of astute intelligence with a knack for the 'ultimate' conversation stopper. Once faced with a howling mob shouting, 'Thatcher OUT! Thatcher OUT!' he said to them, 'Why?' One thing is for certain, Margaret Thatcher has always said that she could not do without him. Indeed, a great fear lies among her colleagues that she would not be capable of continuing should anything serious happen to him. The same powerful dilemma she experienced during Mark's disappearance would be likely to recur – this time challenging her instinctive role as a wife.

Comfortable with the strong support of family harmony, Margaret Thatcher is able to incorporate virtually all of her energies into running the country. Certainly the nation has almost become a wider extension of her family. Every ministry is individually important to her. She is disconcertingly knowledgeable about the activities of every one of them; and is genuinely content to plow through yet another Red Box. Every paper needs her attention, and she gives it meticulously, scribbling in the margin. Letters from the electorate, great or small, are sifted through and a surprisingly large number are set aside for a personal reply, often with a handwritten postscript. She has always placed great emphasis on personally handling her correspondence. Any crisis among her colleagues will warrant a letter. Victims of national disasters – the bereaved and injured afflicted by terrorism, tragedy or war – receive personal letters, not a formal note of sympathy from a Prime Minister but a letter that is full of her own genuine feeling.

Relations with her Cabinet colleagues took some time to settle down. To begin with, she not only had to overcome chauvinism but she also faced the natural resentments that any new leader attracts. After all, Margaret Thatcher is a very feminine woman who likes men, their company and, perhaps (let's face it), even shining among them – if they are witty, good humoured and even faintly flirtatious all the better. At the end of a dinner at No. 10 she remains with the male guests for brandy and has been known to say tongue-in-cheek, 'Shall we now join the ladies?'

The fact that Thatcher is no hatchet-faced Golda Meir but an attractive woman with an obvious sexuality makes acceptance of her leadership all the more difficult for some men. She has never been afraid of her femininity, and her ability to retain her immaculacy while sliding easily between the roles of mother, wife and Prime Minister has often been described as disconcerting.

Cecil Parkinson, one of those who knew how to handle her combination of femininity and strength, tells of the day she discussed the textile industry and a complicated, worldwide arrangement for a textile and multi-fibre agreement. Cecil said, 'She would relate it to buying material herself. She described how she'd been out shopping the week before to buy some material and noticed different foreign fabrics in the shops. Why were they coming here? What was their attraction? In short, she was relating an everyday activity for millions of housewives to a multi-fibre agreement. It was the ability to switch from the abstract to the everyday that is unique.' No Prime Minister has ever approached problems with the same down-to-earth approach.

With her very femininity came a certainty – issues were seen as black or white – never grey. The fact that she is a woman made it difficult at first, particularly for men, to stand up to her without appearing to be rough. They had been taught to be polite to a woman, which acted, to a certain degree, as a restraint. Even Neil Kinnock, who has attacked her viciously and personally over the years, admits that as a woman she is more difficult to oppose.

Throughout the first few years she was very aware she was a female leader among men. It later became of secondary importance and today it is not an issue at all. She has, however, always enjoyed a tough argument. In the first three years of her premiership, there was constant tension in the Cabinet. Margaret Thatcher was still working with the team she inherited from Ted Heath, and they tended to be consensus rather than conviction politicians who were not enthusiastic about her financial package which inaugurated a severe bout of high unemployment.

Arguments round the Cabinet table verged on being bitter and almost bloody. Margaret Thatcher, with her back to the wall in defence of her position, fought the only way she knew: she went on the attack and startled the Cabinet members with her aggression. One frequently unhappy sparring partner, Jim Prior, who never accepted her philosophy, has been pretty blunt, 'She had a degree of efficiency and no-nonsense about her, and up to a point, a ruthlessness in a strange sort of way.' In short, many found her a bit of a bully, with the ability to cut grown men down to size.

One former Cabinet minister, David Howell, was never entirely sure that rough, tough argument was the best path to decision making. As he said, 'If argument was the currency, then argument there should be; but of course, some arguments just left such acrimony and ill-feeling that I can't believe they really could have been enjoyable . . . I find it very difficult.'

The fact is that, even at the best of times, she can be irritable with wafflers; cutting people short in mid-sentence if she disagrees – her interruptions can be terse and quite often rude. A certain icy smile can polish off the meeting. And if a minister

Top, Inner Cabinet gathers in Chelsea after winning the General Election. *L–R,* Angus Maude, MP, Rt Hon James Prior, MP, David Atkinson, MP, Lord Thorneycroft, Mrs Margaret Thatcher, MP, Sir Keith Joseph, Lord Carrington, Francis Pym, MP, Sir Ian Gilmour, MP, Sir Geoffrey Howe. *Bottom,* Margaret Thatcher shares a glance with Lord Carrington in the House of Lords.

does particularly well, perhaps mollifying a hostile television interview, there are no plaudits or effusive 'thanks yous' – good work is expected.

Certainly the first eighteen months to two years of her premiership were particularly unhappy. The early Cabinet meetings were fraught with emotional strain – and conflicting approaches.

Colleagues saw that Margaret Thatcher, standing up to the internal dog fighting very well, was nonetheless under stress. She never complained, never commented, but it was evident – there was no exuberance – her very silence said everything. Ten years later, with the experience and a Cabinet who are wholly in tune with her ideas, there is a totally different atmosphere. As Cabinet Minister, Scottish Secretary Malcolm Rifkind says of the current meetings, 'Today they are positively fun.'

The atmosphere is buoyant: there is a triumphant track record and nowadays the Prime Minister, not previously given to telling jokes, will even crack one against herself. Half-way through the morning she always remembers to call for coffee. In the meeting room the Prime Minister sits with her back to the mantlepiece above which hangs the picture of Britain's first Prime Minister, Lord Walpole. Ranged round the long oval table is the Cabinet team. The meetings are no longer wasted by insoluble debate; Margaret Thatcher and her ministers have a similar mission – they lay their cards out on the table and simply choose the best way to proceed. The harsh

Below, **T**he front room at No. 10, filled with flowers from around the world for Margaret who was recovering from an operation to her hand.

words of ten years ago have softened, perhaps mellowed. But many a colleague remembers how vitriolic Margaret Thatcher can be. Senior politicians and Civil Servants have been left feeling stunned and undefended after a painful and public blast by Thatcher.

One who never recovered from her tongue-lashing was the late Lord Soames who did splendid work taking Zimbabwe through its first elections. But as Lord President of the Council and Leader of the Lords, he fell out of grace while handling the Civil Service pay dispute. He was never a close colleague of Thatcher's and with a reputation for being the rudest man in politics their clash was inevitable. He came out of his final meeting with Margaret Thatcher unemployed. 'I have never, ever, been spoken to by anyone like that in my life,' he said, reeling with shock. He had not, by all accounts, been diplomatic, having insisted that the Private Secretary leave the room and then freely giving her a piece of his mind. The incident was upsetting for Margaret Thatcher, as she has never found sacking easy and his emotional response was hard to deal with.

Loyalty ranks high on the Prime Minister's list of cardinal qualities. It is something she demands from those around her and wholeheartedly embodies herself. The people that she trusts and works closely with are supported on all accounts. Betrayal does not sit easily – nor has it ever been accepted.

When her friend and driver George Newell died, her first thought was for the

Carol Thatcher tenderly fixes her mother's hair on a helicopter trip to the Midlands during the 1979 Election tour.

widow, Mary. She somehow managed to push her timetable around and get to the funeral and continued to ask after her by note or by telephone. For Christmases to come she enquired at the Newell household, assuring herself that Mary was not alone.

Christmas at Chequers has always been an essentially private occasion but Margaret Thatcher is also acutely aware the holiday season is not a pleasant time to be alone. Therefore when she heard that Gordon Reece was on his own after his wife left him, she promptly invited him to join the family. The same invitation applied to Keith Joseph when he parted from his wife. Bachelor Ronnie Millar is a favourite and regular guest. One year a senior Civil Servant whose wife had just died was invited, although she hardly knew him and was quite rankled by the fact that he was a well-known Labour sympathizer. Sir Laurens van der Post and his wife have been on the Christmas guest list for years as has Margaret Thatcher's doctor, John Henderson, and later her mentor Tim Bell.

Chequers runs itself, but on Boxing Day Margaret takes charge. She broke an old custom by refusing the staff's invitation to have a Christmas drink in their quarters before sitting down to their own dinner. 'No,' she insisted. 'You must join us in the drawing room with my guests, then we will serve you and see to the clearing up!' A running buffet is set up for a wide selection of friends; from showbiz to political, her friends from all walks of life are invited.

Prime Minister, employer, wife, mother, politician, friend – she handles each of her roles capably and with flair. Her popularity and her passion for life and leadership are unprecedented. Perhaps it is the fact that she is so complex and yet so focused that explains her success. Whatever it is, she's doing something right.

Autumn at Chequers.

Overcoming any obstacle, including a barbed wire fence during a country walk at Chequers in 1980.

CHAPTER FIVE
THE CRISIS YEARS: 1979–83

Adecade of Margaret Thatcher's premiership has seen both highs and lows and it is a tribute to her determination and focus that she weathered so many storms in those early years. The Prime Minister was faced with the most divided and probably the most unhappy Cabinet of this century. The situation may not have been publicly obvious, particularly at first; however, internal dissension there certainly was.

Her team of conviction politicians were in key posts: namely Sir Geoffrey Howe; and Chancellor of the Exchequer, John Biffen; Chief Secretary to the Treasury, Sir Keith Joseph; Industry Secretary, John Nott at Trade; and David Howell at Energy. Future 'dries' were waiting in the wings at ministerial level: Cecil Parkinson, Norman Tebbit, Leon Brittan, Nicholas Ridley, Nigel Lawson and Tom King.

Around the Cabinet table sat senior heavy-weight politicians who supported different views from those that Margaret Thatcher envisioned. Loyalists to the Heath ideology, their members ranged from Jim Prior, Lord Whitelaw, Lord Carrington, Norman St John Stevas to Peter Walker, and many more. Perhaps she was over anxious to assert her control – mindful of their opposition, and numerically outnumbered by the 'old guard'. Passions rose high. In retrospect it is, of course, far easier to acknowledge that the anguish, wrangling and dissatisfaction could have been spared by more subtle handling of the group. But at the time, not only younger but also supportive of an entirely new philosophy, Margaret Thatcher was faced with a challenge that was formidable. The primary targets had to be the conquest of inflation and the first steps towards trade union reform.

The initial internal problem boiled down to the fact that the 'wets' were invariably disrespectful and sceptical of Margaret Thatcher's belief that there had to be a full-scale change in the management of the economy – tinkering piecemeal diminished the Thatcher strategy. She was seeking radical, revolutionary changes and her critics compounded the difficulties in implementing such measures by grossly under-estimating the Prime Minister's determination. And they were startled and distrusting of the speed with which she wanted to implement changes. Perhaps they could not understand that her determination had developed into a moral crusade: Britain had suffered long enough. Changes had to be made – and made immediately.

Prime Minister Margaret Thatcher leaving for the House of Commons with her PPS Mr Ian Gow, MP. The Falklands War was just underway.

To conquer inflation, which was galloping at over 20 per cent during the overlap with the Callaghan Government, required a steely nerve and a well-thought-out package of remedial bills. Margaret Thatcher also knew that economic recovery was the crucial key-point to the success of all her other policies and it therefore commanded top priority in her work schedule.

To fight the soaring cost of living there had to be a two-fold programme. The sheer supply of money in circulation which prompted inflation in relation to the amount being earned was staggering. In essence Britain was living beyond her means, her citizens relying too much on Government money entering the economy through the public sector spending programmes. The borrowing levels were at an all-time high. There was little 'real' money being generated. So stage one meant the banks had to restrict the amount available for borrowing by raising the interest rates. As companies were forced to pay out more for their loans, they had less to invest and expand. The under-efficient, over-manned and under-productive collapsed and went bankrupt throwing, as it finally transpired, over 3 million out of work.

Every night, television broadcasters tabulated the latest figures for numbers of companies going under. Regional maps were brought out to illustrate visually where collapses occurred, indicating the number of workers involved. All over the country, small, medium-sized and large companies fell. With stage one just underway, and with a large proportion of the workforce, at all levels, seeking Government support, the Thatcher Government cut back the public spending programme by a massive £1.5 billion. In the first Budget under the new government Sir Geoffrey Howe took out the scalpel – making cutbacks that were admittedly extreme and severe. The effects were biting and a state of national hardship ensued. People from every walk of life protested bitterly. In an attempt to encourage incentive, however, income tax was reduced from 33 per cent to 30 per cent and over one million people taken out of the taxable bracket. As the cold winter set in, a state of near panic grew among the 'wets' of Margaret Thatcher's Cabinet.

Through unprecedented and severe policy, Margaret Thatcher did, however, set the ball rolling for the new enterprise economy. She had cut back the dead foliage to allow a new prosperity to germinate. It would take time. Direct taxation was down but indirect taxation went up – increasing VAT from 8 per cent to 15 per cent. Essentially she was giving people the power to choose how they wished to spend their money. These were early days, however – the spending boom had not yet begun.

Every department was hit, ranging from the Civil Service shedding 100,000 jobs to Michael Heseltine cutting a swath at the Department of Environment – 15,000 jobs in total were lost. The Ministry of Defence axed a further 24,000, and the list went on. Social Security, however, remained unscathed – it had to – there were too many to take care of. Those who were panicking in the Cabinet wanted to ease the financial pain on families out of work: delaying the new policies for a while in order to undertake more Government spending programmes, thereby mopping up some of the huge flow of unemployed.

Some were disillusioned by her lack of response to their pleas. Jim Prior puts his finger on the general feeling: 'Margaret, Geoffrey and Keith really had got the bit between their teeth and were not going to pay attention to the rest of us at all if they could possibly help it.' Thatcher's degree of concern was not the issue, but rather, they queried whether the short, sharp shock of monetarism would really work. They feared civil disorder and future electoral defeat – Margaret Thatcher was convinced that this was only short-term agony – the price for longer term success.

Added to their problems was the fact that Britain was also embroiled in a world recession, due mainly to the price of oil doubling. Although this situation meant cheaper fuel, the price of Britain's North Sea oil, an important source of revenue, fell in return. In any case, it was appalling to see Britain belittled as a weak country with no trading influence or standing. Countries like Germany, devastated by the last war, were leading Europe; France had a dynamic economy; Britain stood pitifully as the third poorest nation in Europe.

At her first Conservative Party Conference in October 1979 Mrs Thatcher warned, 'The work that the new Conservative Government has begun is the most difficult, the most challenging that has faced any Administration since the war . . . Yes, the Conservatives can do it. And we will do it. But it will take time. You gave us your trust. Be patient. We shall not betray that trust.'

Interestingly she was fully aware of the stress that unemployment and collapsed businesses were having on family life. She noted, '. . . the strength of the family is truly tested. It is then that the temptation is greatest for its members to start blaming one another and dissipating their strength in bitterness and bickering.' She understood that it was a time when families needed back-up and she was determined they would get it.

The years 1980 and 1981 brought little comfort. Pay increases which helped fuel inflation were still far too high – in the public sector they remained at 20 per cent. Her target was 6 per cent – a figure that, at that time, appeared to be sheer romanticism. And as more companies collapsed, output decreased, causing national income to continue its slide. Margaret Thatcher knew the pressures the nation was facing and she made clear her agenda of hope and direction for the future. She added, 'We have to move this country in a new direction, to change the way we look at things, to create a wholly new attitude of mind . . . it is time to change people's approach to what Governments can do for people, and to what people should do for themselves; time to shake off the self-doubt induced by decades of dependence on the state as master, not as servant.'

By the time of the 1980 Party Conference in Brighton, the Prime Minister was all the more determined to coax and encourage her people along. First, however, she dealt tartly with hecklers trying to burst into the hall. 'Never mind, it is wet outside. I expect they wanted to come in. You cannot blame them; it is always better where the Tories are!'

On a more serious note she urged party members on to 'a new independence of spirit and zest for achievement'. She required cool nerve to stay on course, and as a warning note to any faint-hearted constituents who sought reverse action, she stated firmly, 'The lady's not for turning.'

The landscape may have been bleak but the seeds of positive change were sown:

the public were feeling the effects of tax cuts, along with the attack on inflation and public spending, and the trade-union relations embarked on the course of change. The policies affecting the trade unions were the start of a long process which would later culminate in the showdown with Arthur Scargill several years later. The first issue at hand was the question of a man's right to be free of the small minority in his trade union who imposed their will to insist on a strike against majority interest. Up and down the country, men and women were being physically threatened if they disagreed with their trade union bosses. It was not a class war between workers and management but rather a fraternal war amongst the workers themselves. The country was grinding to a halt through strike action, largely brought on by the coercion within the movement. Secret ballots had to be brought in and secondary picketing of businesses not involved in the disputes had to be outlawed.

It is little wonder that Margaret Thatcher had acquired so much support – many disenchanted Labour supporters had voted Conservative for this reason alone. If they dared to cross picket lines they risked losing their union card and job. The problems came to a head when the Post Office strike, costing taxpayers over £110 million, was brought on by only 150 people who made the decision to strike against the wishes of the others. The two-day-week strike by the engineering union cost the industry £2 billion in sales. The chances of making up the sales were grim – the Germans, the Japanese, the Swiss, the Americans – all benefited from the British lack of productivity.

One of the innovative reforms that Margaret Thatcher imposed was the revolutionary idea to give council tenants the right to buy their homes at a competitive rate, with 100 per cent mortgages. The principle of a property-owning democracy had been around for a long time, but it took Margaret Thatcher to pick it up by the scruff of its neck and make it a reality. Could she ever have imagined that ten years later council estates across the nation would become rainbow bright with the new Georgian doors and baskets of flowers belonging to their proud new owners? In a decade, over one million households took advantage of the scheme. Although the Socialist councils were determined to block these democratic rights to home owners, the Thatcher Government managed to remove and identify every obstacle that they presented. By 1988, there was even an innovative scheme for entire housing estates to become independent.

Margaret Thatcher, who came into No. 10 Downing Street on such a wave of enthusiasm and excitement, had slipped impossibly low in the opinion polls. Indeed, there is no record of a premier who had fallen so swiftly and so far in public confidence. With the budgeting problems at home organized, at least in theory, she turned her attention to Britain's contribution to the European Community. The practical housewife that made up a good part of Margaret's character pounced. Why was Britain contributing £800 million a year and receiving nothing remotely similar in return? she demanded.

Quite ignoring diplomatic niceties and horrifying the Foreign Office who had spent years delicately tiptoeing the diplomatic rostrum, she went to the Community Summit saying, 'I know nothing about diplomacy, but I just know and believe that I want certain things for Britain.' The Foreign Office, to their peril, did not take her

Top, The Young Socialists demonstrate against Mrs Thatcher during the Young Conservative Conference at the Compress Theatre in Eastbourne. *Bottom,* Health Service workers led by Alan Fisher protest against the Conservative Government in Brighton.

seriously at the beginning. They believed she would soon fall in the customary language of conciliation. Not so: they were astonished when she turned down the first offer of a one-off rebate of £350 million – quite unsatisfactory she called it. She wanted fundamental change and she was going to wait for it. The European leaders were aghast – while it had been perfectly acceptable in the past for France's General de Gaulle to plead national interest first, they never expected Mrs Thatcher to follow suit. She was not playing the game according to their rules. Giscard d'Estaing, the French President, called her 'La fille de l'épicier' (the grocer's daughter).

The angry tussle with the European Community did, however, bring fundamental changes. Six months later Margaret Thatcher won her point. Britain was refunded £1,800 million, with respect to her contributions in 1980 and 1981, and the EEC undertook to devise a new and fairer system.

The world, in particular Europe, were becoming aware that Britain had a leader of rare and determined quality. Perhaps one of the most fascinating insights into the flexibility of Margaret Thatcher's mind appeared when dealing with the creation of a new constitution for Zimbabwe. Although the Prime Minister was characterized by her unshakable direction and purpose, she was not inflexible as was demonstrated when she turned her attention to Zimbabwe.

Thatcher favoured the resignation of Bishop Muzorewa and the formation of an Ian Smith regime which gave majority rule to the blacks, but with some important positions of power for the whites despite the fact that Lord Carrington, her Foreign Secretary, saw this would not go over well in world opinion. He persuaded her to examine other courses, and four months later she accepted Lord Carrington's suggestion with the enthusiasm of a missionary. There would be a Constitutional Conference in London at Lancaster House which would involve equally all political parties of Zimbabwe. A new constitution that satisfied all parties was hammered out. The irony was, of course, that these events led to Mr Robert Mugabe's, an avowed Marxist of the ZANU party, becoming the first Prime Minister. As this result became clear, pressures were brought against Margaret Thatcher to 'adjust' the new situation. To her credit, her answer was 'No'. The die had been cast, she said, and we must live with it. The principle of one-man, one-vote elections had been accepted. If Mugabe won, so be it.

It was a triumph – on Mugabe's election victory, Mrs Thatcher and Lord Carrington received plaudits from all over the world. The Rhodesian/Zimbabwean elections and the European Community battle illustrated that the Prime Minister of Britain was tactically astute. She may have been a conviction politician standing by her decisions but under no circumstance did that mean she was blindly dogmatic. She could combine firm resolution with a cautious evaluation. These talents would again become particularly evident when she faced the Falklands campaign.

The Zimbabwe negotiations were not, however, without tensions. Halfway through them, Margaret Thatcher flew to Lusaka for the Commonwealth Conference where she was greeted by an unsympathetic and disapproving audience. As she flew out on a RAF VC10 with Lord Carrington, he noticed that she was nervously nursing an outsize pair of sunglasses with particularly large lenses. She explained, 'It's in case they got rough and start throwing acid in my face.' Later, despite nasty experiences with demonstrators and a totally disorganized press conference where she appeared profoundly shaken, she had not donned the glasses; she defiantly appeared without protection, 'I am damned if I am going to let me see I'm afraid,' she barked.

Former premier James Callaghan had a sage piece of advice for his Foreign Office ministers: 'Never forget that it's never the big foreign affairs problems which cause real trouble. It's the pimples at the other side of the world which start wars.' How right he was. Few of Margaret Thatcher's Cabinet had spared a thought for the Falklands, unsure of exactly where they were or the consequences of Argentina's sovereignty claims.

It is hardly surprising that the Argentinians miscalculated Britain's interest in the islands for they were just windblown, treeless and rather inhospitable outcrops in the South Atlantic, and Britain's world standing had sunk to rock bottom. Prime Minister James Callaghan had plunged Britain's chaotic economy ever further into difficulties and because he was unable to manage his domestic problems, London was bypassed for powerful capitals like Washington, Bonn and Paris. Britain had little international recognition and because postwar history has shown Britain shedding colonies as quickly as she could; the Argentinians did not take seriously the threat of Britain reclaiming the islands. They had been blowing the warning whistle of their ambitions for years, but Britain had paid little attention to the significance – ignoring the alarmed warnings of a union diplomat in Buenos Aires. It was a situation that developed through Argentina's miscalculation of Britain's growing role in international events and, of course, her new, determined Prime Minister.

The last straw came when, in the interests of cutting the defence spending at home by a mere £2 million a year, the HMS *Endurance*, the ice patrol ship operating in the Falklands waters, was withdrawn. Fundamentally, this cutback served as an invitation to the Argentinians. The idea that Britain would one day be at war with Argentina was, at the time, laughable. As General Galtieri told the Americans, 'The British won't fight.' The British reputation was one of malaise, she was hardly expected to have the strength or the will to fight. When Margaret Thatcher finally received a telegram from the British ambassador in Buenos Aires, she found it sufficiently worrying to write on it, 'We must make contingency plans.'

But it was too late – the Argentinians landed their scrap merchants on South Georgia and erected their flag. That first step accomplished, the Argentinian fleet was reported to be steaming towards the Falklands. Their expected landing date was Friday morning, 2 April.

Margaret Thatcher took the prospect of invasion very seriously. She rallied a War Cabinet together and dispatched three nuclear-powered submarines as a holding operation – it was a somewhat belated gesture for they arrived in the South Atlantic a week after the first major landing by the Argentinians had taken place. Throughout that week the atmosphere around the Prime Minister, in and out of Downing Street, and her room at the House of Commons, was thick with tension and unspoken disapproval – Britain was militarily impotent, facing humiliation by a 'tinpot dictator'.

The man who was brought in to lift and encourage the team was not a politician but Admiral Sir Henry Leach, the First Sea Lord and Chief of Naval Staff. His first appearance caught everyone unaware. He arrived fresh from a naval ceremony dressed in full regalia. Somewhat comically, however, the glory of his appearance failed to impress the duty policemen at the House of Commons who banished him to a bench in the public hall where he remained until spotted by a horrified junior whip.

For Margaret Thatcher, he was her lifeline. It was a meeting of minds and purpose which saw them both through what could have been a disastrous campaign.

Opposite, **M**argaret Thatcher leaves 10 Downing Street after a meeting with her Inner Cabinet to discuss the latest Argentinian developments. *Top*, Tank Force personnel at firing practice in the Southern Atlantic. *Bottom*, Islanders watch as Royal Marine Commandos hoist the Union Flag on the Falklands. 1982 (*Press Association*).

Defeat would have culminated in her, the Prime Minister's, resignation and for him the disintegration of what remained of the navy. That morning in the Cabinet meeting Margaret Thatcher's first words were very calm and controlled: 'Gentlemen,' she said. 'We have to fight.' Faced with the massive logistics of fighting a war 8000 miles away, Leach took the positive view, one which remained with him throughout the military planning. 'It *can* be done,' he said.

No landing of men and munitions can take place without a naval force; this justified the navy's very existence which, until then, had been in doubt. It would be feasible to mobilize a Task Force to leave, within the week, on 5 April. First, however, Britain had to suffer the humiliation of the Argentinian landing on the Falklands on 2 April. The next morning Parliament was reconvened on a Saturday for the first time in twenty-five years. It was not Margaret Thatcher's most glorious moment. Members were in vindictive and outraged moods and she knew it. Uncharacteristically, Thatcher's speech that morning did not carry its usual undefatigable fire. It was hesitant and read partly from a script prepared by the Foreign Office.

She did, however, clearly spell out her own message: of the 280 Falklands islanders she said, 'They are few in number but they have the right to live in peace, to choose their own way of life and to determine their own allegiance.'

Above all, she stressed that Argentina had taken the islands by force. There was a vital matter of principle at stake – there was no point in giving in. The Falklands were and still are under British sovereignty no matter how the Argentinians wish to see them historically. During that last week, however, there had been frantic, behind-the-scenes attempts to persuade the Argentinians to withdraw. Even President Reagan had spoken to General Galtieri personally – but without success.

It was time for action. Margaret Thatcher had thought out the options – and remained firm to her objectives. Her whole philosophy and being were attuned to standing up to aggressors. She announced the departure of the Task Force. Further internal upheavals followed. Lord Carrington resigned as Foreign Secretary. He felt he had no other choice, although Margaret Thatcher tried hard to persuade him otherwise. His department had been held responsible for failing to detect the Argentinians' mood and determination soon enough. He also paid the price for years of prevaricating by the Foreign Office who led the Argentinians to believe that there could be 'lease-back' discussions on the Falklands.

The new Foreign Secretary, Francis Pym, was not ideal from the Prime Minister's point of view – particularly because their styles and methods were so different. There was little empathy between them and as time went on relations became something of a strain. He was, however, a senior politician and highly experienced.

In the lull that took place before the landing of the Task Force a fever of diplomatic activity continued, in an attempt to seek a peaceful solution. Shuttle diplomacy began when America's Secretary of State, General Al Haig, the self-appointed international emissary, intervened, attempting to bring about a negotiated peace.

Of the British Prime Minister he had no doubts. She was going to stand her ground. This battle was not just about the Falklands but about Britain's international standing and pride. Britain could not appear to collapse in the face of petty aggression – it would have devastating consequences.

A diplomatic victory was secured at the United Nations and Britain's rights were enshrined in a UN resolution – Resolution 502, which called for the 'immediate withdrawal' of Argentinian forces, was passed as a prelude to negotiations. Equally importantly, Margaret Thatcher was able to draw on Article 51 of the United Nations Charter which approved the inherent right of an individual to collective self-defence in the event of an armed attack. Effectively, this sanctioned all of Britain's subsequent actions that took place over the next ten weeks – her case was justified. Ironically Margaret Thatcher, who has never been an enthusiastic admirer of the United Nations, blessed them for this course of events.

And so the War Cabinet – made up of Defence Secretary John Nott, Deputy Premier Willie Whitelaw, Foreign Secretary Francis Pym and Party Chairman Cecil Parkinson – provided the political will for the military experts to get to work. For them Margaret Thatcher was the perfect leader. She carefully weighed up the options, made a judgement and stuck by it. In short, she was a decisive leader who did not vacillate. As the Chief of the Defence Staff, Admiral Sir Terence Lewin, said later, they were able to 'put the case to her, and say this is how it is, this is the decision we want. We want it now and we want it quickly and we don't want a wishy-washy decision, we want a clear-cut decision. She was magnificent in her support of the military.'

Having never personally witnessed war-time action – its sheer bloodiness, horror and degradation – she was able to deal more effectively, without being blinded by emotional considerations. It was therefore necessary for her colleagues to prepare her gently for what would follow.

For others who had experienced war-time service, like Lewin who had served on the Arctic convoys to Russian ports, and Whitelaw and Pym who had both been awarded the MC, this war naturally evoked vivid memories. They took it upon themselves to prepare the Prime Minister emotionally for the casualties and deaths that would follow.

On 2 May she gave orders that the Argentinian cruiser *General Belgrano* be torpedoed by a British submarine. Ian Gow, her Political Parliamentary Secretary, came in to see her later that night. 'Will it sink?' she asked.

He replied, 'If it is hit below the waterline, it will sink.' The Prime Minister, aware that the men aboard were human beings, even if they were the enemy, said hopefully, 'I suppose the survivors will be picked up. . . .'

In fact, 368 members of the crew perished. Hard on the heels of this attack Margaret Thatcher, while chairing a meeting in the Cabinet Room, was brought the news that the HMS *Sheffield*, a well-armed Type-42 destroyer, had been hit by an air-launched Exocet missile. Exploding into a burning inferno it had to be abandoned, but twenty men died and of the remaining crew members many had been seriously burnt and maimed.

For the rest of the evening, colleagues feared for their leader. She was herself a wife and mother and her heart was heavy with anguish for all those who had died –

CONDOR
TROOP-RE
GET ME
HAM

5   9
OMMAND O. RE
RULE
RITANNIA

RECCE TROOP
59 IND. CDO SQN
WE WENT
WE FOUGHT
WE CONQUERED

it was as if the young men had been her own. She became physically withdrawn and pale – as she concerned herself with the wives and family of the deceased. In Willie Whitelaw she confided, speaking rapidly and emotionally, 'What are we going to do? What can we do for these people? Oh dear, oh dear, oh dear, I do hope they are all right . . . do you think they will be all right?'

One of the many moments when the big, comfortable Willie became a shoulder for Margaret to lean on – he had the ability to reassure her and above all gently advise that as a leader she must keep her fears to herself. With him she could share her worries, but her generals must never see a moment of weakness or self doubt.

The last diplomatic initiative failed on 18 May, and Margaret Thatcher gave the go-ahead to the Task Force waiting in the icy waters off the Falklands. The winter was setting in and, with freezing winds and sub-zero conditions, the campaign would have to be a quick one.

It was a time wrought with emotion. As the weeks went on, with helicopters plunging into freezing seas, ships going down, soldiers being shot or running into land mines, there was plenty to weep for. A deadly phase had been reached.

Fourteen ships were either hit, and damaged or sunk. In all 250 men died. Margaret Thatcher sat down every night, no matter how late, and as the reports came in, handwrote a personal note to every family who had lost a member. It was a message from her heart; despite extreme exhaustion she was driven: the families came first. During the day her thoughts remained 8000 miles away. She constantly waited for news to come through – wondering and worrying about details as minor as the weather in the Falklands. 'It is clear down there', or 'The weather is terrible', she'd mutter as she read local forecasts. By night she sat by the telephone waiting for news. Because of the time differences, they were often very long waits – especially to call America. Her most constant worry was that the Task Force ships, especially the two precious aircraft carriers, might be sunk – bringing the whole operation perilously close to a disaster. In keeping with the sombre times she wore dark clothing. The agony never eased – two supply ships, the *Sir Galahad* and the *Sir Tristram*, were hit; with fifty-six men killed and forty-six atrociously burnt and wounded.

But the Task Force, after a landing at Carlos Bay, began to push their way slowly over heavy bogland towards Port Stanley. The day of the invasion, Margaret Thatcher was in her constituency. 'I knew the invasion was under way and that I couldn't cancel anything. I had to carry on and I knew that I couldn't get home until the invasion was complete; and when we got back home the action was complete. That was marvellous; and we did not lose any ships then. But later, when they came to bomb, bomb, bomb, that's when we also had a very depressing time.'

The weeks ground by, until finally there was triumph. As one officer reported, 'Suddenly we saw all these specks running off. . . .' Half an hour later a white flag was seen flying over Port Stanley. The next day the Argentinians formally surrendered. The fighting was over.

Outside Downing Street, the press gathered. The crowd cheered and sang 'Rule Britannia' when the Prime Minister appeared. Her expression was one of sheer relief that it was all over: 'Rejoice,' she said simply. Her words have since been misconstrued to be gloating over the Argentinian defeat. Not at all, as she later explained: 'I felt colossal release . . . It was the most marvellous release I had ever had when the news came in. It was a day I dreamed of and lived for. And when the surrender was confirmed . . . then I knew that whatever the problems and troubles, I would have in the rest of my period of office, they were as nothing then and now.'

In fact, from that moment, Margaret Thatcher's standing soared upwards – before the Falklands War her rating in the polls stood at 25 per cent; with the victory safely in the nation's pocket, it soared to 59 per cent. Her recovery had begun gently before the campaign began; the economy was beginning to show some signs of light. However, it took her achievement in battle to convince the electorate they were in safe hands. Her public appeal lasted a long time in the aftermath of the war. On the world stage she received similar recognition – she had become a more visible and influential power. She had illustrated to the entire world that she could *and* would stand up and fight for freedom.

Previous page, British Troops arrive in Portsmouth; the Falklands War is over. *Above*, Margaret Thatcher, who spent 80 minutes aboard HMS *Hermes*, decorates the officers. This was her first personal greeting. (Martin Cleaver, *Press Association*)

CHAPTER SIX
THE 1983 ELECTION

The Falklands victory fed Margaret Thatcher with the momentum she needed to push towards the General Election the following year. First, however, there were some hurdles to overcome. Creeping up almost unexpectedly was the effective and highly emotional anti-nuclear campaign orchestrated by the Left, and in its wake they whipped up anti-American suspicions over Britain and NATO's nuclear weapons policy. It was focused on the proposed deployment of Cruise missiles at Greenham Common as part of a twin-track agreement under which NATO would press for deployment if the Soviets withdrew and SS20s on deployment would follow. Scant regard had been paid, however, to the Soviet buildup of SS20s targeting on Europe, an unprovoked new generation of missiles which threatened the balance of forces between East and West. Massive demonstrations organized by the Campaign for Nuclear Disarmament both in central London and at Greenham Common were set on the agenda as the prime issue in the General Election. They were calling for one-sided Nuclear disarmament.

Ironically the 'Nuclear Election', as the campaign came to be called, was a blessing in disguise. The silent majority rose up in outrage. This was one issue which the people across the country would never tolerate – the surrender of personal security and with that, freedom. One-sided nuclear disarmament was such an affront to the sensibilities of the average Englishman that it was hardly surprising that when I set up the Women for Defence (later to be known as Families for Defence) it was swept along on a tide of nationwide support. It was a head-on challenge to the anti-nuclear protesters – making clear that they could not in fact be defined as a peace movement – and Margaret Thatcher whole-heartedly supported it. She has always liked the idea of direct action taken by individuals.

Unwittingly it served a second purpose. The nuclear debate distracted the public from what was expected to be the key election issue – an unemployment figure of 3.5 million. Unemployment was high and still rising. Programmes for retraining were in their infancy and industrial output was lower than it had been for twenty years. Attempts to bring order in trade union reform were considered insubstantial and ineffective. Among other schemes the reform provided Government funding for union ballots on wage disputes – but not on the key sensitive areas of compulsory secret ballots before strike action, the election of top union officials and strikes taking place before dispute procedures had been implemented. For the ordinary trade unionist, Labour or Conservative, there was much more to be done. Mrs

Top, Victory night, June 1983, at the Conservative Party Central Office with Cecil Parkinson and his wife, and Denis. *Bottom,* A champagne celebration at Finchley headquarters for her 1983 victory.

Top right, Margaret Thatcher visits her old school in Grantham. *Bottom right,* Margaret Thatcher with TV personalities at Wembley for the 1983 Tory victory rally. *Top,* The 1982 Party Conference in Brighton with Cecil Parkinson. *Bottom,* Campaigning in Finchley.

Thatcher had been cautioned by Jim Prior about going too far, too fast, and she had taken his advice. More legislation would follow as the trade unions became acclimatized to the change.

On the face of it – not a very promising start to the General Election. Few expected 9 June to be the overwhelming triumph it turned out to be.

At the outset of the campaign the signs were encouraging for the Conservative Party. They led Labour by 12 per cent – and Margaret Thatcher sought an election at the earliest possible opportunity. She could have delayed it by one year; but as she explained, with Britain in a perpetual state of election jitters, the economy, the pound and thus the country suffered. Certainly, Margaret Thatcher was buoyant, and when her daughter Carol teased her about the possibility of returning to Flood Street, back came the retort, 'I have no intention of needing Flood Street.'

True to form, her family rallied round Margaret – Carol flew back from Australia where she was working as a journalist and took over as her mother's right-hand assistant *and* wardrobe mistress. It was a comfortable arrangement which gave Carol the rewarding task of assisting and providing emotional support for the Prime Minister. Curiously, domestic arrangements were still very ad hoc and informal after four years at No. 10. Still without a resident housekeeper or cook, the shopping and cooking was done throughout the campaign by Margaret Thatcher's secretary, Joy Robillard, Carol or one of the two faithful cleaning women.

Margaret's wardrobe was handled personally by herself or Carol and, as always, her clothing was indicative of her fashion sense and beautifully organized. Throughout the years, Margaret's clothes have become more stylish and in her tenth year of high office, she was reckoned to be one of the world's best dressed women. Her growing confidence in herself allowed her to break out of the safe but somewhat dowdy mould of little suits with bow blouses. Designer Susan Small who dressed Princess Anne became the first favourite of Margaret and eventually other designers were discreetly asked to send clothes round to No. 10. The biggest hit finally turned out to be Aquascutum who devised a complete wardrobe of highly stylish clothing that incorporated fashion and yet dignity. Everything from dazzingly cut coats, pill-box hats and dramatic evening wear found their way into her wardrobe. In 1983 she had reached the halfway mark to complete elegance, and, as she demonstrated to Carol, she categorized her clothes according to the occasion. In cupboard one, she kept dark executive suits with a suitable mix of blouses, along with comfortable shoes for walkabouts. Cupboard 2 held her best shoes for speech-making and campaign-trail clothes. Cupboard 3 was full of clothes suitable for television appearances, while cupboard 4 contained dresses for evenings and rallies, carefully categorized by colour, fabric and style. Margaret also received dental treatment to remove the small gap between her two front teeth.

Margaret Thatcher found it refreshing to be back on the campaign trail, travelling around the country by every mode of transport from campaign bus to helicopter. Walkabouts, speeches and rallies were perfect opportunities to meet people – an activity

Opposite, Margaret and Denis Thatcher wave after the 1983 Election Victory.

Opposite top, **C**onservative Party celebrations at Finchley headquarters. *Opposite bottom,* Denis and Margaret celebrate together at Finchley. *Top right,* Polling day, 1983; Margaret Thatcher leaves Flood Street. *Top left,* During her election tour, Margaret stops to do some shopping in her Finchley constituency. *Bottom right,* First time at the Cenotaph with defeated leader of the Labour Party, James Callaghan. *Bottom left,* Opposing views at the hustings in Finchley.

she has always loved. Hecklers and demonstrators were greeted with equal grace – she quite liked having things livened up! As long as she was assured of having a loudspeaker with which she could be heard over their voices. As she said, 'Your own people then love it – they have something to cheer against and to cheer for.'

As far as she was concerned, it was utterly natural to be the first Prime Minister of this century to be running for a second term and, as she admitted after four years of running, the life suited her: 'I've always been used to working hard.' She has never been one to crave quiet moments of relaxation; or somewhere to rest the soul. She has no hobbies to speak of, although she does take an interest in decorating and flower arrangements. She has very few personal non-political friends and naturally has little time for idle chatter. Her family are her personal relaxation and she finds their company in her spare time restorative. Rest for Margaret Thatcher is curling up on a sofa late at night with some political cronies, whisky and soda in her hand, to philosophize about where they are today and what the future holds. Switching off simply means changing from one political topic to another. Politics are relaxation for her – she is continuously spurred by her innate curiosity and zest to tackle the next subject.

The election campaign had its high and low points, as did all of the previous campaigns. The message and issues were, however, the same as ever. As she said, it was all about 'defence, jobs as part of the economy, putting the facts on the record on the welfare state and home ownership. Home ownership is tremendously important and people in council estates have had the opportunity to buy for the first time.'

It was true enough – as she toured the country the torrent of welcome came from all classes, especially her new, often first-time voters: the working classes. Nothing surprised or irked her more than when the Labour Party accused her of encouraging a class war. For the girl from a grocer's store in Grantham, it was a misplaced accusation – and quite beyond comprehension. Whatever might be said about her weaknesses, social snobbery was never one of them.

Daily press conferences at Central Office invited recriminations that she was being 'head mistressy' as she dominated the proceedings, answering questions for her colleagues. It might have irked them, and in particular Francis Pym, who on one occasion was slapped down for suggesting that too great a majority for the Conservative Party might be undesirable. On the whole, the country loved it and Margaret Thatcher was unapologetic for her style: 'I am what I am. I do believe in trying to persuade people that the things I believe in are the things they should follow. . . .'

Low points were reached when Denis Healey, deputy leader of the Labour Party, accused the Prime Minister of 'glorying in slaughter', adding, 'She is wrapping herself in a Union Jack and exploiting the services of our soldiers, sailors and airmen, and hoping to get away with it.' Uproar followed and ultimately irreparable damage was wrought not only to Healey but also to the Labour Party campaign as a whole. Coupled with the Labour Party's stance on one-sided nuclear disarmament and the bitter divisions it brought with it, Healey's comments only worsened their position. Labour's own former premier, James Callaghan, brought further trouble upon himself when he argued against it.

Labour's declaration that Britain would become, 'the first nuclear weapons state to renounce unilaterally such weapons' sent shivers down their supporters' spine; and Neil Kinnock furthered the damage a few days later. In response to someone at a conference who shouted 'Mrs Thatcher has guts', Kinnock said, 'It's a pity that people had to leave theirs on Goose Green in order to prove it.'

In short Labour was being buried by accusations that they were unpatriotic – a subject that the British have never discussed until pushed. Indeed, for years afterwards, despite attempts of the Labour Party to adopt the rose as their emblem, they never were able to reassure their countrymen that they would put their country's security first. It became an irksome mantle which they still have not, to this day, been able to shed.

As a finale, during her last party political broadcast, she took the opportunity to hammer her points home. Having convinced the nation that the economic medicine had to be injested, she ended with the words, 'May I suggest to every citizen of our country, every man and every woman of whatever political persuasion, that on Thursday you pause and ask yourself one question – who would best defend our freedom, our way of life, and the much-loved land in which we live? Britain is on the right track. Don't turn back.'

Meanwhile the polls were encouraging. Despite the unemployment factor, victory was almost inevitable. This time round, the night of the count was much calmer. That super-charged tension of 1979 had given way to a quiet confidence, but the inevitable unease that comes when results begin to pour in was sparked as they sat down to the usual high-speed supper in the Downing Street attic flat. Party chairman Cecil Parkinson joined the family and chatted quietly to Margaret for a few moments before departing for his own Hertfordshire constituency, while Margaret Thatcher set off to Hendon Town Hall for the declaration of her own results. A long night lay ahead of her – it was well past 4 a.m. when she arrived at Central Office and celebrations had already started. The Parkinsons, Sir Geoffrey Howe and Lady Howe, her Parliamentary Private Secretary Ian Gow, his wife and others were holding a champagne toast to her. Dawn was breaking and at 5 a.m. on 9 June, Prime Minister Margaret Thatcher returned to No. 10 Downing Street, the first premier in this century to be elected for a second term of office without a break – and to compound the compliment, she had won it with a substantial majority.

Admittedly, it has been stated that the 1983 election was not so much won by Mrs Thatcher as lost by her opponents. Maybe that statement holds an element of truth but her majority was evidence enough to ascertain the real truth: the British people were beginning to pick themselves up; to find a new confidence and to become aware that with Margaret Thatcher a positive programme and hence new life lay ahead.

CHAPTER SEVEN
CHANGING A NATION

It is often said that Margaret Thatcher's first Parliament served a purpose to set the scene: to condition and train the country to accept change; to break old, bad habits; to adopt a new self-reliance; and to take the new opportunities with both hands thus avoiding the clutches of defeatism. These were early days yet, but the election victory gave the signal: a new era had begun. It would take the whole of Margaret Thatcher's second Parliamentary term to achieve the turnaround that she so clearly envisioned but which was still a dream for many. Even those who were not entirely sure of her could never doubt that she represented movement, challenge and change – it was difficult to avoid being swept along with it.

Quietly and steadily the economy was moving. Inflation tumbled from 1980's all-time high of 21 per cent to 4 per cent in 1983 where it lurked, with only a few blips until it headed towards 8 per cent in late 1988.

But the first job to tackle, before the nation could really be released for the big surge forward, was the unfinished business with trade union reform. Looming in the foreground and representing militant totalitarianism was the President of the National Union of Mineworkers, Arthur Scargill, a self-confessed Marxist. Miners both feared and revered him. He ruled his kingdom with an iron fist; and the hesitant voice of reason by any of his men was met with brutal intimidation.

Margaret Thatcher had been waiting for her moment with Mr Scargill for a long time – she was not to be disappointed. Two days before the General Election, Scargill declared war against Margaret Thatcher. His declaration was imbued with a hatred that fuelled the subsequent battle and was monitored by his political sympathies in Moscow – *Pravda* followed him with interest. His opening salvo was to warn workers that they could not expect any protection from the Government and in consequence they would have no alternative but to turn to 'extra-Parliamentary action'. The re-election of Margaret Thatcher, he said, was 'the worst national disaster action for 100 years'. In short, he wanted to bring down the Prime Minister and her Government.

He warned that unemployment would reach 8 million and predicted 'social violence on the streets, aggravated by a paramilitary police force'. And so he declared, 'We must resolve to fight in the trade unions and all other democratic bodies inside and outside Parliament to bring about another general election as quickly as possible to be rid of this vicious Government.'

His intentions were certainly never disguised by a velvet glove. He made his views so abundantly plain that Margaret Thatcher was immediately on the alert. He may have thought he would rock her, but he totally under-estimated her determination to fight him – and to win. The miners may have won their battle with Edward Heath,

Top right, The Police block a section of the MI during Miners' flying pickets arrival from Yorkshire in Nottinghamshire pits. *Top left,* Ian McGregor, Chairman of the National Coal Board. *Bottom,* Miners in South Wales signal 'V' for Victory as they head back to work after the strike.

but times had changed, and so had the players. Margaret Thatcher had taken time to prepare for the confrontation. She had no doubts about the fact that she was dealing with a Marxist revolutionary. If Scargill wanted a strike, so be it – but he would lose, for the Government had been building up coal stocks for years. At long last the way would be clear for the trade unions to be relegated to their proper place.

As a first step, Scargill declared an overtime ban, and then, as he had failed three times in the past to get the miners to agree to a strike by ballot, he did it his own way. He used flying pickets, intimidation, physical assault and threats to close the pits

by force. The first mine closed was in March. Scargill pressed that the Government's intention to reorganize the coal-mining industry and close uneconomic pits, despite generous compensation, was unreasonable. Economics did not come into it, as far as he was concerned, it was class warfare – it was 'we', the beleaguered miners against them, 'the Government'.

Forces that he had not bargained for rose up against Scargill. The miners who did not want to be bullied did not support the strike; they demanded the freedom to continue working. The Nottingham miners led the way for repressed miners and formed the breakaway union – The Union of Democratic Mine Workers. Mrs Thatcher brought in Ian MacGregor to take over as Chairman of the Coal Board; he was a tough negotiator but invariably low key. Tempers flared when he was faced with the intractable, volatile and powerful orator in Scargill who knew how to use the media – and had attracted full coverage.

Although Margaret Thatcher never personally met Scargill, and indeed left the daily grind to MacGregor, she gave him full back-up with police forces drawn from all over the country. Scargill tried to blame the police for the fighting, but ultimately the public could see for themselves that, were it not for the pickets encouraging bloody confrontation, there would be no need for the police intervention. A climax came when miners dropped a block of concrete on a taxi cab driver, David Wilkie, which killed him. It was not the only casualty of the war but it was symptomatic of the levels the violence had risen to.

Throughout the time Margaret Thatcher spent meeting with her advisers at Downing Street she was acutely aware of the support Scargill was receiving from the Soviet Union and Libya. Estimates taken by the Secret Service estimated that his financial support had reached a figure of £7 million.

By 1985, almost one year after the confrontation had begun, Scargill was forced to call off the strike – by that date more than half of his workforce had returned to work anyway. In all, the showdown had cost the country £3 billion. But Margaret Thatcher had no doubt that it had been worth every penny. Not only could she reassert the 'right to manage' industries but ultimately it meant that trade union relations could be put on a new footing. For the country to become and remain prosperous she had to be at peace in her own trade union relations. A working partnership had to be developed. Eric Hammond, leader of the electricians' union, the EEPTU, blazed the trail for team work, implementing no-strike agreements and democracy for the workers, which hitherto had been just a dream for some unions. The days when unions, as Hammond put it, would be 'led by donkeys' was over.

Margaret Thatcher's second Parliament had the semblance of a continual battle. This term, as illustrated by the Scargill confrontation, battles focused on extreme socialism from within – the desire of some to destabilize Britain and forcefully establish lawless Marxist kingdoms. Hard on the heels of the mine dispute was the battle with Labour-controlled town halls which had, in some areas, developed wide-spread

Top, New Conservative MPs after the 1983 Election Victory, Queen Anne's Gate Club. Centre, Arthur Scargill, President of the NUM. Bottom, Margaret Thatcher with her favourite team cast of 'Yes Prime Minister', Nigel Hawthorne and Paul Eddington.

corruption and spending programmes which were quite irrespective of the ratepayers' needs or indeed of their support. In all some 174 local authorities, all Labour controlled, declared themselves 'nuclear-free zones', thus establishing the right to pursue a programme which had nothing to do with local services as such. They embraced a bewildering bunch of causes ranging from anti-racism, nuclear disarmament, homosexuality and lesbianism, ecology, pro-Sinn Fein movements to peace studies.

Two halls, in particular, led the movement: in Liverpool, Derek Hatton led the Militants on a stampede unheard of previously, virtually bankrupting the city by 1986. In London, on the Greater London Council, Ken Livingstone spent a massive £8,876 billion for what he admitted was his own declared aim, 'to use the Council machinery as part of a political campaign both against the Government and in defence of socialist policies'. London boroughs like Islington, Lambeth, Brent and Hackney were local leaders while Manchester followed suit.

Such abuse of tax-payers' funds went against the grain of everything that Margaret Thatcher stood for. She could see the country being torn apart from within and thus, in 1984, the Government set to work curbing the free spending. Unfortunately, heavy weather was made of it; and a poor presentation of the case meant that the opposition had a field day claiming that any curbs were 'anti-democratic'. The first Government step was the Rates Act of 1984 which made it illegal for a local council to set rates above a certain level – this bill came to be known as 'rate capping' and was viciously attacked. The hatred came from all sides, for well-behaved Conservative councils were also affected – and they bitterly resented it.

Margaret Thatcher dines with members of the Jewish community in her Finchley Constituency.

It was not a happy time for Environment Minister Patrick Jenkin, who was handling it. By nature he was not overly aggressive; and urging him on from behind was the Prime Minister who said 'rate capping' did not go far enough. The municipal councils, an unnecessary top tier, should be abolished altogether. The storm unleashed by the opposition was stupendous – Ken Livingstone rushed headlong into a vastly expensive advertising campaign (at ratepayers' expense) before finally disappearing in a blaze of fireworks, which was again at ratepayers' expense (costing some £250,000) in 1986.

Young Socialists expressing their opinions on the sands of Scarborough during the Young Conservatives Conference.

Unveiling the Yvonne Fletcher Memorial in St James's Square, London.

Top left, **M**ark Thatcher joins his mother for a birthday celebration at the Young Conservative Association's Ball in Brighton. *Top right*, Margaret Thatcher takes the opportunity to visit a Dulwich factory during her election campaign. *Bottom*, Reception at No. 10 for Conservative members of the trade unions.

It was a battle only partly won. There still remained local borough council spending programmes which gave them the freedom to spend without being fully accountable to the community. Only one in four actually paid rates. Town hall reform had still some way to go and more public relations storms were lined up for Margaret Thatcher's next Parliamentary term when she set into motion a replacement of rates with a 'Community charge'. To be paid by everyone with very few exceptions, it was an unpopular move and inevitably initiated a war of public retaliations. The opposition, seizing at the last vestiges of local power, called it a 'poll tax' with a vociferous campaign suggesting that it was an outrageous burden on the poor. It was a battle worth running. Margaret Thatcher knew that in the long run, when the dust had settled and the new community charge had been put into action, the country would take it in its stride. At last town hall politicians would have to be accountable to the ratepayers.

The real test of leadership for Margaret Thatcher was, however, still to come. The test appeared in the form of terrorism, a regime that had been seething and multiplying for years rooted in the historical divisions in Northern Ireland. Whereas in the past there had been a justifiable cause for complaint by the Roman Catholic minority in Protestant Ulster, the picture changed when the IRA used it as a convenient whip with which to beat the British Government. The paymasters of the crusade were largely the Marxist Libyans. The aim of the IRA has little to do with improving the lot of the Ulster people; it has become an unabashed attempt to destabilize a democratically elected Government using brutish methods of hit-and-run murder. Over the years there has been a steady build-up of terrorism. By 1984 over 1,000 innocent men, women and children had been murdered; some were British soldiers who were, according to the IRA, a legitimate target; many were revenge killings that slayed innocent bystanders. At present, casualties are estimated to be in the 20,000 region.

There was seemingly no limit to the bloodshed. Then came the Conservative Party Conference of October 1984 at the Grand Hotel in Brighton.

It was Thursday night. All evening the party faithful had been cheerfully weaving in and out of parties, dinners and receptions. Lord 'Alastair' McAlpine held his usual lobster and champagne party in his suite at the Grand. Finally the bars emptied, leaving just the very hardy to finish their drinks.

Upstairs in her suite at the Grand, the Prime Minister, still in her ballgown, was seated at her desk, her Party Chairman, John Gummer by her side. It was 3 a.m. when she finished her conference speech; and she reached out for just one more paper to work on. It was that insatiable drive to work that probably saved her life.

Had she retired for the night, she would very likely have been in the bathroom preparing for bed. From beneath the floorboards of the room below her a huge explosion roared through the building, blowing her own bathroom completely out and bringing the entire centre of the hotel down – from top to bottom.

The Prime Minister was entirely unscathed – a matter of a few feet in the wrong direction and it might have been different. Luckily, Denis had finished in the bathroom and was already safely in the bedroom. In the aftermath of the explosion there was a terrible silence, then the building began to crumble – an avalanche of stone, furniture and personal belongings cascaded in a whirl of blinding dust. In its wake lay a terrible toll of casualties. Among those killed was the wife of the Chief Whip, John Wakeham; Norman Tebbit and his wife Margaret were badly wounded – she is paralysed for life. The final tally made one thing clear – the bomb was intended to eliminate the Prime Minister and her Cabinet with one stroke.

For Margaret Thatcher it was the beginning of a nightmare. Swallowing her personal anguish over the crisis, she summoned up from the depths of her soul the strength and adrenalin to keep going and to give leadership and support.

Immediately following the blast, she did not break down, did not scream and did not panic. Realizing at once what had happened, she allowed herself to be led

Opposite, top right, **T**he Grand Hotel, Brighton, the day after the bomb exploded. *Top centre*, Firemen, rescue and clean-up crew flood the beach following the bombing. *Top left*, Some of the rescued party members sit on the bench at the sea front. *Opposite, bottom right*, The Party Conference continued, but the atmosphere was sombre. *Bottom centre*, Lady Diana Neave, wife of the late Airey Neave escapes from the hotel in her nightdress. An IRA bomb had killed her husband several years previously. *Bottom left*, Margaret Thatcher wipes away a tear as she emerges from the church near Chequers after a service for the Grand Hotel victims.

down a back staircase and be driven off by police to their station at Lewes. She was accompanied by Denis and Sir Ronald Millar, who had just walked out of her room when the explosion hit them. As the building crumbled, he had, for some reason, clung desperately onto the conference speech and he carried it with him then.

Margaret Thatcher finally slept for only two and a half hours. Anxiously pacing her room, she finally convinced her colleagues to allow her to visit those in hospital. Somehow her clothes had to be rescued (her ballgown was hardly appropriate) and even without her personal grooming tools, she managed to emerge looking quite business-like – if only on the exterior.

There was a strange feeling of normality as she walked into the Conference Centre; although at that point only half the assembly had got through the security checks. Yet those who saw her applauded. She looked well put-together but, not surprisingly, somehow different – strained, if very collected.

Behind the scenes, Margaret Thatcher's script writers were feverishly rewriting her conference speech. The original version would never do. As Sir Ronnie Millar said, 'I looked at the speech with Stephen Sherborne. There was a big section knocking Kinnock and the Labour Party. After the Labour leader's sympathetic words on the bombing, it would never do to leave it in. With the help of Robin Butler, we three sat behind the scenes of the conference hall. By twelve noon we were in the thick of it, and by 1 p.m. were working hard with Margaret. Just then the news came through that four bishops had come to pay their condolences to her. It just could not have come at a more awkward time as we were racing against the clock.

'Margaret was marvellous. She broke off. Rushed to powder her nose and tidy up and received them. Then back to work, and somehow we just managed to get it all typed up in time for her to go onto the rostrum at 2.30. It was an emotional occasion. The atmosphere was electric and Margaret herself was in a defiant mood. She had been to see the victims in Sussex Hospital, had talked to Norman Tebbit; she came to the hall in full command of herself.'

She began at full throttle, 'The bomb attack on the Grand Hotel early this morning was first and foremost an inhuman indiscriminating attempt to massacre innocent, unsuspecting men and women staying in Brighton for our Conservative Conference. Our first thoughts must at once be for those who died and those who are now in hospital recovering from their injuries.

'But the bomb attack clearly signified more than this. It was an attempt not only to disrupt and terminate our Conference; it was an attempt to cripple Her Majesty's democratically elected Government. That is the scale of the outrage in which we have all shared, and the fact that we are gathered here now, shocked but composed and determined, is a sign not only that this attack has failed but that all attempts to destroy democracy by terrorism will fail.'

They were strong words. Prime Minister Margaret Thatcher was back, in full control of herself, and able to vet her anger with sharply directed words.

Two days later the shock inevitably set in. She attended Matins at Chequers Parish Church and the tears welled up. As she explained, 'The shaft of sunlight came through the stained glass windows; I suddenly realized this was a day I was not meant to see.'

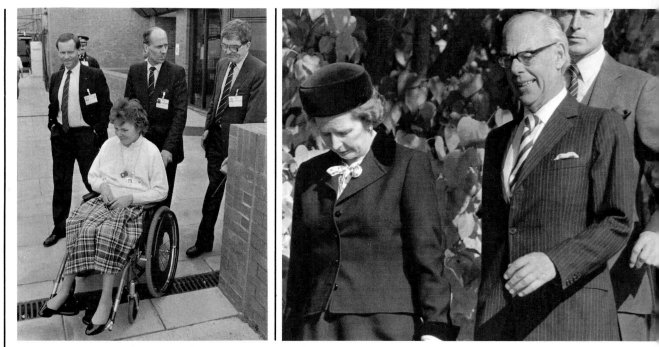

Top right, **T**he anguish is obvious as Denis and Margaret Thatcher bow their heads at a memorial service for the Grand Hotel victims. *Top left,* Norman Tebbit's wife is wheelchair bound as she attends her first Party Conference since the IRA bombing in Brighton.

The whole episode had a profound effect on Margaret Thatcher, perhaps deeper than she expected. It certainly explained her redoubled efforts to ensure that terrorism is abolished – to prove that it cannot pay. Those at the receiving end of her efforts have been stunned by the vehemence of her insistence on global co-operation to tackle terrorism. She called on her good friend President Ronald Reagan to help in the extradition of terrorists and to block funds flowing to the IRA from America. In turn she rounded on her European allies insisting on the same high standards that she held herself.

While the European Community gave her their support, in practice, their pledges were somewhat weak. In 1988 a furious row broke out when the Belgian Government refused to extradite IRA terrorist suspect 'Father' Patrick Ryan who was wanted on charges of conspiracy and explosives charges. Instead the priest was returned to the Republic of Ireland which in turn refused to arrest him. As a result bitter words flew between allies, straining what is remaining of the Anglo-Irish Agreement. Margaret Thatcher knew then as she knows now that if there is to be any abolition of terrorism – the scourge of the modern world – it has to be a battle in which all countries are united. There can be no frontiers in this battle.

By 1985 Margaret Thatcher was able to sit back and look, for the first time, at the fruits of her labours. Her first years were dominated by trade union reform and controlling inflation. With unemployment dropping fast to almost half the 1980 level, and income tax down to 25p in 1988, a financial boom ensued. The news that now dominated front pages and television headlines was the city and financial reports.

Businessmen as well as men and women who had never taken to business, found they had a flair for enterprise. Suddenly the country became aware that boom times had arrived. The times gave rise to rocketing successes – new millionaires, new prosperity and a spending power previously unknown. It did, however, give rise to something else – city scandals.

Cleaning up the city became part and parcel to setting the scene straight for Margaret Thatcher's personal vision – 'A Britain where everyone has a financial stake and a commitment to Britain's success.' The first stage in accomplishing her vision had taken place in 1979 when she brought forward home ownership and the right of council tenants to buy their own homes – it was a winning policy. Every Englishman and woman dreams of owning his own castle – it imbues one with dignity, status, pride and confidence. Not only were dismal estates transformed but investment in the home reached an all-time high with new kitchens being installed and homes crowned with new décor. By May 1989 Margaret Thatcher could proudly boast that this scheme has enabled well over one million people to buy the homes they never dreamt possible.

This was just the beginning. In her second term of office new words crept into her vocabulary: 'popular capitalism' – the selling of State assets. It came to be known as 'privatization', one of the pinnacles of her achievement, or as it has often been called, the 'flagship of the Thatcherite fleet'. So successful have been the sales that overseas countries have been fascinated. Privatization programmes modelled on Britain's experience have been adopted by France, Italy, New Zealand, Malaysia and Jamaica.

As practical as ever, Margaret Thatcher could immediately see that the best people to run an industry were the experts in that field, not Civil Servants or the Government. In turn, private ownership would encourage better and more efficient management. There would be no unnecessary drain on Government funds; with the added bonus of money for the Exchequer, less income tax would be necessary – it was a scheme that would attract millions of votes from the first-time shareholders. In short, she wanted to bring big business to the people, to make them feel involved in a part of Britain's prosperity. Big business was not the reserve of gigantic financial institutions – Thatcher would make sure it was available for all.

Of course there had to be opposition and indeed an element of sour grapes. Former Prime Minister Harold Macmillan, on his maiden speech in the House of Lords as the Earl of Stockton, accused her of 'selling the family silver'. This jibe hurt for Mrs Thatcher had great respect for Macmillan; and had indeed sat at his feet for a photograph at the Carlton. This time she felt he was out of touch with modern times. Tactfully she kept her silence.

In short, privatization has become the core of Margaret Thatcher's new society. The sales had officially begun with British Telecom in 1984 although, in fact, the National Freight Corporation had discreetly led the way in 1982 when it sold the business back to the management and employees; and British Aerospace in 1981, which served as a less-publicized trail blazer for the big launches.

Some privatizations were conducted with all the razzmatazz of a circus. Pressing the public to understand that share ownership meant everybody could purchase and at prices they could afford, the launching of British Gas was one of the most successful, with its teasing advertising campaign: 'Tell Sid. . . .' They did and 4.5 million applied. The taste for privatization had been whetted – the shares issue was vastly over-subscribed and the public thirst became unquenchable.

It reached an unprecedented level. Ordinary men and women who had never dreamed of owning a share certificate found there was no mystery involved in buying one; it was an easily managed task and through this action the face of Britain changed. The proportion of the population owning shares in 1979 when Margaret Thatcher became Prime Minister was just 3 million. Today, a decade later, it is over 9 million. In effect, the proportion had risen from just 7 per cent to 20 per cent – a staggering rise representing a vastly different Britain. Britain now has become the biggest property-owning democracy in the world, ahead of America, Germany and France.

By now a new mood had enveloped the country. It had become ultimately respectable to work hard and to seek reward for effort. There was nothing shameful about enjoying the proceeds. Inevitably there were envies sprung among those who would like to see a return to Big Brother Socialism – the opposition talked about the north/south divide, the rich getting richer and the poor getting poorer. The facts, however, belie these sentiments. As Margaret Thatcher moved to celebrate her decade, Scotland, once the bed of high unemployment, soared ahead with a prosperity based on high technology. Her reputation has become so widely known that the mid-belt of Scotland is now known as 'Silicon glen'. And across the rest of Scotland (albeit a map covered with red dots denoting the growing number of Labour MPs), there has been a dramatic increase in living standards. Any service industry will happily describe new orders – for example, orders for expensive pine kitchens have soared. In Glasgow, the financial sector has a zip of its own. And indeed, Glasgow, under the Government enterprise zone scheme, has long lost its dank, slum-like living standards in favour of middle-class aspirations.

In London's East End, the Isle of Dogs has been transformed by the freedom that the 'enterprise zone' has allowed developers. Bright, futuristic office buildings are leaping up; the old warehouses have been converted into luxury apartments; and elegant houses are being spawned – and through that, the developments have given local populations new jobs and homes at prices they can afford. All around the nation these developments have sprung to life. In the northwest Michael Heseltine, while Environment Minister, transformed Merseyside. Indeed, it is likely that his Merseyside developments, with parks and leisure centres, were the torch-bearers for the developments to come.

This new energy, harnessed by Margaret Thatcher, has given rise to a term borrowed from across the Atlantic – the 'yuppie'. The yuppie factor, derided as selfish and uncaring by the critics, was the very element that gave Britain its activism. A Thatcherite yuppie is just as likely to be an East End barrow boy as an Old Etonian. He or she can be a member of virtually any class, linked together with his or her fellow yuppies by enterprise and ambition, and is smartly trendy – certainly not an intellectual. Education could either be university – or rudimentary. One thing is certain: he is a socially mobile fellow in a hurry – cordless telephone stuck to his hand and accustomed to taking holidays that are exotic but short. She will be equally ambitious, forging her way into business with a ferocity that impresses her fellows; she will delay marriage and children and put a high price on good-quality clothes, sleek car and designer home.

CHAPTER EIGHT
DOES SHE CARE?

The most popular jibes against Margaret Thatcher have been those that portray her as an uncaring, driving personality, intent on power and pushing her policies forward, irrespective of the effects on others.

This could not be further from the truth. Those who work closely with her will maintain that, if anything, she cares too much, too deeply – to such an extent that she carefully analyses today's problems, and looks ahead to a certain degree in anticipation of policies she should tackle. Admittedly it is not her style to pause and plan the general strategy that will take us into the future – forward-looking speeches have never been her style. She is sustained by a general vision of a nation she wants; a horizon she is aiming for, the details come later.

The urgency and speed with which she works is derived of caring. Her work ethic supports her theory that not a moment must be lost for there is much to do, and she has to supervise it. It is just as well that her stamina can reach exceptional levels. The fact that she can sustain herself on an average of four or five hours sleep a night has become a legendary and much-envied feat. It is normal for her to work on her boxes until two or three in the morning and be up again at 6.30 a.m. She can sustain an intense pace that leaves her colleagues gasping. But at the end of the day, the truth is she does get tired, extremely tired. Her stamina is a perpetual triumph of spirit over flesh. She drives herself extremely hard – partly out of a second nature inherited from her father, and partly because she does not want to leave anything to chance. She knows every department intimately – often to the embarrassment of her ministers. She absorbs her papers in the Red Boxes with relish. Everything is noted, comments jotted in the margin and remembered. She will recall word by word a conversation from months back when the speaker – to his peril – was sure she was not paying attention. She will nonchalantly retort, 'Well, you did say that to me. Now, how does that square with what you are saying now?'

Her ability to absorb information has meant that throughout Whitehall her presence is intimately felt; unlike her predecessors who operated within their immediate spheres and left it at that. Some might say she interferes too much in departmental decisions that properly belong to her Cabinet ministers. She pays, perhaps, obsessive attention to detail; however, there's no denying the fact that her methods of housekeeping do work. She can proudly claim that she is more aware of how her programme is going than anyone else. She alone has access to the complete picture, is therefore the sole person capable of taking an overview. Such attention to

Margaret Thatcher greets the neighbourhood children after a Young Conservative Conference in Scarborough.

detail is illustrative of her vigilance. Furthermore, she has the unique and some-what humble ability to evaluate political concepts through the practical eye of a housewife.

Margaret Thatcher's solicitude is evident by her prioritization of issues. Perhaps somewhat surprisingly, issues of national importance can often take the back seat to issues dealing with the human factor. At a meeting about peace studies in schools with discussions about political indoctrination and bias, her first words were, 'I have been meaning to deal with this for some time now. I am so glad you have come. This is the time to deal with it. In fact let me just tell you about a letter Denis received from a history master in Putney. . . .'

To Margaret Thatcher caring often means not letting people down. She sets her priorities according to what she best thinks the country needs. For instance, her commitment to controlling inflation was not affected by the lack of popularity that ensued. Her supreme certainty that she is doing right is often misconstrued as bullishness; however, it is certainly indicative of her belief in her ideals and aims – aims that she has developed for the welfare of the nation and the people. It is her practical and down-to-earth approach that is most illustrative of her conscientiousness. When accused by her European counterparts for being undiplomatic in her fury over the freeing of 'Father' Patrick Ryan, who was wanted on terrorist charges, she replied 'I don't care how undiplomatic I may sound. I only care about Britain. . . .'

By instinct, she is a home-supporting person – and it is her fundamental belief that the family is the foundation of our civilization. Having such experience, she knows the strength of a good family – her faith in Victorian values: hard work, thrift and personal responsibility have become the core to even the most political of her philosophies. Her belief in personal responsibility sparked her programme to give families the freedom and the ambition to care for one another rather than depend on the State: a dependence that often brought malcontent, loss of confidence and initiative, and purpose. By using the family as the basis of her concern, she found that her priorities, after dealing with the economy (which affected every family), were domestic concerns: the improvement of education, the health service, housing and, finally, the environment.

It was her support and encouragement that gave impetus to the Education Reform Act of 1986, which was designed to improve standards, and to give greater freedom to parents. She was often criticized for her decision to take the sharply high-profile and voluble Edwina Currie aboard as a Junior Health Minister. Mrs Currie may have made some colleagues wince, but to Margaret Thatcher she was just the answer. Edwina's strong, articulate voice warning of health hazards that ranged from fatty foods and drink to lack of exercise forced the nation to sit up and listen. The choice of Mrs Currie for the role represented Margaret's concern about the nation's health. Similarly, Thatcher has directed her attention to the future funding of the Health Service ensuring that quality service is available to all. As more expensive and sophisticated treatments become available, she finds ways to make them cost-effective and available to anyone who seeks them. She seized upon the most radical ideas, like the opting out of hospitals, to keep her programme going.

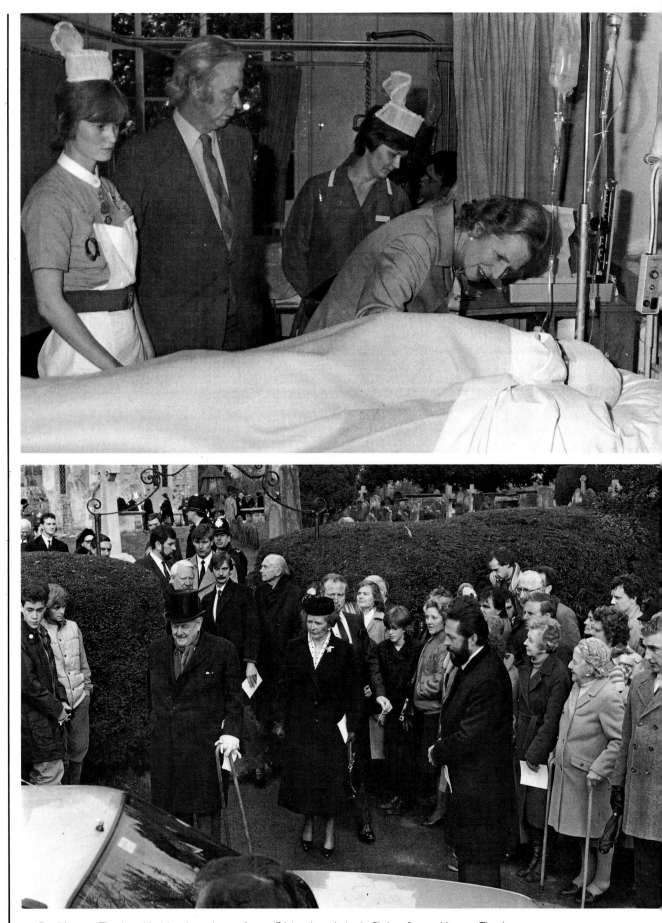

Top, Margaret Thatcher visits injured guardsmen after an IRA bomb explosion in Chelsea. *Bottom*, Margaret Thatcher attends the funeral of the Earl of Stockton as Lord Hailsham, Sir Alec Douglas Home and the new Earl of Stockton look on.

With regard to housing concerns, although the right-to-buy scheme was an overwhelming success she was not wholly satisfied. Her goals expanded to include better deals on the management of council estates; greater freedom of choice for the tenants; and increased opportunities to restore run-down estates to pride-worthy homes.

Margaret Thatcher's ability to startle her audiences is never-ending. As Cecil Parkinson once said, 'It is her insatiable curiosity and interest. She still has tremendous enthusiasm . . . that is the secret of her success.'

Perhaps her enthusiasm for an ever-increasing circle of issues was most pronounced when she addressed the Royal Society and expressed her concern for the environmental issues like a committed Green. The 'Greening of Mrs Thatcher', as it

Top, **M**argaret Thatcher visits a School for the Blind in Exeter. *Bottom*, Lord Tonypandy greets Mrs Thatcher at the Savoy Hotel Lobby Journalists' lunch.

came to be called, initially provoked sceptical laughter, but it did not last. With political dexterity, she had snatched the mantle of the left-wing, green lobbies and put it on her own shoulders. At the Conservative Party Conference in 1988 in Brighton she said 'We do not have the freehold to the earth,' she said. 'We have a lease. . . . The last thing we want is to leave environmental debts for our children to clear up – slag, grime, acid rain and pollution.

We will join with others to seek further protection of the ozone layer – that global skin which protects life itself from ultra-violet radiation.'

They were not just words; she meant what she said. Only months later, her latest junior ministerial recruit – Virginia Bottomley, the Under-Secretary at the Department of the Environment – called a one-day conference on the environment.

Margaret Thatcher canvassing during the 1983 election, in her Finchley Constituency.

Protection of the ozone layer was top of the agenda. The definition of caring has often been misconstrued to mean an anguished wringing of hands. This has never been Margaret Thatcher's style. To her, caring means taking practical decisions fast and getting things done. For her, caring equals results.

Within her personal life, however, caring takes on a more tender definition. One of the reasons she inspires such loyalty from her team is that she works very closely with them – taking a personal interest in them and their families.

Her attention to detail has always inspired fierce loyalty. The Conservative Party Conference in Brighton in 1978 coincided with her fifty-third birthday she was presented with a huge cake and a Paddington Bear. Whisking them back to the Grand Hotel, she threw a party for the policemen who had been guarding her, then arranged

Top, Margaret Thatcher visits old age pensioners in the young Sir Winston Churchill's Constituency in Stratford.
Bottom, Visiting Rochester School during the 1987 Election tour.

to transfer the cake and bear back to London for a birthday party taking place the next day for one of her aide's children. Despite her gruelling schedule of the previous week she still took time to concern herself with the enjoyment of others. Only two examples of her typical care for her own team, it's easy to understand why they, in turn, were willing to work long and inhuman hours – glad to do it for her. Certainly money was not the draw.

As one secretary explained, 'Early on in her leadership, before she became premier, one of us would be there, until the House rose or until midnight, which ever was the earliest, and I would drive her home, so tired I could barely speak after a hell of a long day . . . but we always knew she had to go home and start on her boxes. She never had anyone on her staff who could have worked harder than she did . . .

Top, Hair ruffled by the wind, Margaret Thatcher meets the farmers' wives in Cornwall during the 1979 Election tour.
Bottom, Visiting the local engineering works in the West Country during the 1979 Election campaign.

it is very much easier to give your all to someone who you know is really giving their all too.'

Margaret Thatcher's reputation for kindness never changed. She was always generous about gift-giving and on her first trip to America she managed to bring back a charm for her secretary, Diana Powell's, bracelet. 'I want stars and stripes,' Diana had said teasingly before Margaret Thatcher left. She'd never dreamed that the busy Prime Minister would remember her whim.

Nowadays there can be no shopping expeditions. If she wants to purchase something she must decide in advance and then ask someone to go out and buy it for her. But even then she is very precise. She sent flowers to congratulate her publicity strategist, Tim Bell, and his wife, Virginia, on the birth of their first child, Daisy. Thoughtfully, she had not ordered cut flowers but rather a bright plant which would endure.

Caring often meant a tactful word at the right moment. Naturally, people can feel intimidated in the presence of a Prime Minister but she is celebrated for making people feel at ease. At a dinner for agents she sat next to one gentleman who had been dreading the thought of an evening of deep political analysis. He feared he could not keep up with her. But as he said, 'Not a bit of it. We talked about children – hers and mine – and family upbringing as a whole. She likes children for their naturalness

Margaret Thatcher greets the nursery school children in her Finchley Constituency.

Margaret gives a little motherly advice to a group of school children in Wales, 1987.

and was surprised to hear that the Lawson children do not like playing in No. 11's garden. It is too public, they say, for cops and robbers. "Oh dear!" was her immediate reaction. It was all such an easy evening: I could hardly believe I was sitting next to the Prime Minister.'

On a less highly profiled occasion, she asked one man during a walkabout, 'What do you do?'

'I am only a grave digger, madam,' he replied.

'But it takes a man of dignity to prepare the ground for burial,' she said softly.

To Margaret Thatcher, caring can also take the form of personal, written expression. She frequently sends off letters with a line or two written at the end in her own hand. It could be a comment – or an expansion of a point. It also bears proof to the fact that her letters *are* indeed personal – she despises the American-style Presidential letters which are invariably signed by a machine.

It was not just the Falklands families who received letters from her but also widows of IRA terrorism victims. She never hesitated to fly to Northern Ireland to visit the beleaguered armed forces, the police and civilians who have suffered in the tragedies. In 1979, upon hearing that seventeen soldiers had been killed, she immediately sat down to write to each soldier's family. Letter writing is an outlet for Margaret Thatcher – it allows her to express the deep sympathy and distress that she really does feel for people in duress. It is an outlet to express affection and feeling for her friends.

Throughout less emotional times she would break off during a late night session to query how a colleague would get home or if he or she had eaten.

Her team have always been beneficiaries of her concern. Intensely distressed by the situation, she consistently supported Norman Tebbit during the long months that his wife, Margaret, lay paralysed in Stoke Mandeville Hospital. She even arranged for Norman to stay at nearby Chequers so that he could easily visit his wife.

Margaret Thatcher has always taken the time to confront issues whether they be personal or national. A thought is spared for anything that affects people – for people make up a nation. She has extended a hand across that nation for one reason alone – she cares.

CHAPTER NINE
BANANA SKINS

No Prime Minister, whether he be in power for a short or a long term, can expect to have an administration which works entirely according to plan. Inevitably there are times when things have either been misunderstood or just plainly gone wrong. The wobbles in her premiership have been remarkably few. Some were at the time viewed as being more serious than they actually were.

As the Party was celebrating the 1983 General Election victory, Margaret Thatcher's Party Chairmam, Cecil Parkinson, privately admitted to her that his former secretary Sara Keays was expecting his child. The news could not have come at a more awkward time for Cecil Parkinson, a married man who had steered the Tory Party to a brilliant election victory – a victory in which the issue of family solidarity played an important role. It was a highly emotional period of time. Margaret Thatcher, a happily married woman, could not conceive of the idea that Parkinson would break up his marriage to marry Sara nor could she ignore his previous pledge to do so.

Whatever Cecil Parkinson decided to do, Margaret Thatcher would not take the opportunity to moralize. She understood the pressures that faced politicians – and these happenings were not unknown. Above all, she regarded Cecil as a friend and made it clear that he could rely on her loyalty. She faced a dilemma – could she still keep him in the Cabinet? The answer was yes, but not in the post she had first ear-marked for him – Foreign Secretary. Instead he was given the less prestigious post of Secretary of State for Trade and Industry. It was a hedge against the news becoming public, as it inevitably would.

Ironically, as the storm unleashed by the British press achieved hurricane proportions, outside Britain the reaction was one of total amazement. Could it really be true that in a world where one marriage in three broke down, Britain was so morally outraged by infidelity? In Europe or America such events would bring little comment. Pressure, however, mounted to such a degree that finally, at the following Conservative Party Conference in Blackpool, Cecil Parkinson felt he had no alternative but to resign. Margaret Thatcher agonized for her friend and she urged him to 'sleep on it'. His decision, however, had been made. On Friday, the last day of the Conference, he resigned and immediately drove back to London. He remained politically distant but personally close to Margaret during the next four years. Margaret Thatcher was saddened by the loss. In any case, she wanted to pay tribute to his efforts during the election campaign. She made a point of saying that she would not forget 'the man who so brilliantly organized the campaign'. The text of the speech had to be scanned carefully for *double entendres*, a number of which had to be lifted out. The storm did

Margaret Thatcher looks on with approval as Cecil Parkinson makes his speech.

not fully subside until nearly three years later, after which she was able to reinstate him to her Cabinet in the position of Energy Secretary.

Following her tribute to Parkinson, the next items on the Conference agenda were relations with the Soviet Union and the proposed first deployments of Cruise missiles at Greenham Common in December 1983. She carried a stern word of warning to the anti-nuclear protesters. 'The so-called peace movement may claim to be campaigning for peace, but it is NATO and the Western Alliance which have been delivering peace in Europe for more than thirty years. Peace is hard work and we must not allow people to forget it. The Soviet challenge remains. . . .'

It was a message that she stood by throughout the decade, even when relations with the new Soviet leader, Mikhail Gorbachev, took a turn for the better.

Further storms, however, lay cumulating on the horizon. In 1984 she made a much-applauded visit to Washington where she addressed a joint session of Congress and was heralded by Ronald Reagan, with whom she had struck a very deep and personal working relationship. He said of her, 'World affairs today demand the boldness and integrity of a Churchill. In his absence I know he would want us to look to you as the legendary Britannia – a special lady, the greatest defender of the realm.'

Less than a month later, however, shock waves ran through Britain as the news broke that the United States had invaded Grenada, a Commonwealth country. The invasion was deeply embarrassing for Margaret Thatcher. President Reagan sent in his troops to rescue a small Caribbean state which had been collapsing under the Marxist leadership of Maurice Bishop, a close friend of the Cuban Marxist leader,

Top, Michael Heseltine, who resigned as Tory Minister for Defence. *Bottom*, Leon Brittain, who tendered his resignation after Heseltine's departure.

Fidel Castro. The people of Grenada had appealed for help. He was going to give it to them.

Relations between Margaret Thatcher and Ronald Reagan became very strained. As she explained, 'I am totally and utterly against Communism and terrorism, but if you are going to pronounce a new law that, wherever Communism reigns against the will of the people, even though it has happened internally, there, the United States shall enter, then we are going to have a really terrible war in the world . . . we don't just march in.'

In the House of Commons she faced wrath from all sides. Some said she should have gone further and joined in with Reagan; others felt she should condemn the American President more vociferously. Denis Healey called out at her, 'Reagan's Poodle. It's really time you got off your knees.'

At a time when Margaret Thatcher was trying to win support for the Cruise missile deployment, this situation could not have been more unfortunate – it was fuel to the fire of growing anti-Americanism. And more brewed – 1986 would go down in history as a year of crisis. The trouble began with the row over a small, ailing Somerset helicopter company, Westlands. A debate over whether it should be rescued by an American-orientated Sikorsky deal or by a European consortium brought together and inspired by Defence Secretary Michael Heseltine arose. Heseltine, always a passionate pro-Europe man, cherished a dream of a closer European defence policy, and he saw the opportunity to make it work.

Others, like the chairman of Westlands, Sir John Cuckney, saw the matter differently – from a strictly commercial point of view, they felt that the American offer was better for them.

There the matter should have rested. But personalities of the two men conflicted, ultimately dragging down two Cabinet ministers. Michael Heseltine walked out of a Cabinet meeting and announced to the press outside, 'I have resigned.' He felt he had been misled about the Cabinet's intentions to examine the European offer. Then in the wake of his resignation Margaret Thatcher, who had been determined to stay out of the row – sensing that it should remain a departmental affair – was dragged into it too.

Leon Brittan, the Trade Secretary, was brought in to help Sir John Cuckney advise his shareholders that a letter Heseltine had written to *The Times* contained 'inaccuracies'. The Attorney General, Sir Patrick Mayhew, wrote a private letter on the matter to the Department of Trade and Industry and sent a copy to No. 10 referring to 'material inaccuracies'. The confidential letter was leaked to the press – and fury broke out. Was Mrs Thatcher to blame? Did she encourage underhand behaviour? Was it Leon Brittan himself? Who was it?

In the end Leon Brittan took the rap and resigned, after admitting his department had leaked a private letter. Recriminations that it was in reality Downing Street who should take the rap flew. They in turn suggested that Leon Brittan had seized upon the chance to shut Heseltine up for good. It was a sad and shabby end to the careers of two distinguished Parliamentarians. Heseltine, after twenty years on the front benches, was out of the political scene for what appeared to be forever. Leon Brittan finally resigned his Richmond, Yorkshire, seat three years later and became Britain's Commissioner to the European Community.

The Prime Minister herself was the victim of heavy fire: colleagues maintain that this episode undoubtedly represented the lowest point in her entire decade as Prime Minister. She was faced with a wilful, powerful Michael Heseltine who she could not control. Behind the scenes, manipulation between senior Civil Servants, determining that one view or another should be confirmed, only made matters worse. What affected her most deeply and profoundly were the allegations that she was personally involved in blocking Michael Heseltine's bid and personally responsible for the publication of a private letter that was critical of her Defence Secretary.

To a woman politician who prides herself on integrity above all else, the claims were insulting and hurtful. She became so depressed that she had even mentioned resignation to friends, during a late evening drink the night before the crucial Westlands debate. Public popularity hit an unprecedented low. Her reputation for boldness, honesty and straight-forward dealing was attacked and the accusations were soul-destroying. Her natural talent for shrewdness and firm management were debated and she was publicly portrayed as being both weak and dogmatic. The Conservative Party slumped below the Labour Party and the Alliance in the polls – and despite the windy weather, Westlands stuck to the original offer and took up the American option.

As one observer who was close to the scene remarked, 'She took it very hard. It was undoubtedly her lowest point in the entire decade, more so than during the Falklands crisis which after all was a war. Perhaps the day Mark was lost in the desert was the only one that could match for depression.

'She became very silent and withdrawn. It was perfectly obvious she was deeply unhappy and distressed by the whole Westlands episode. She was also very concerned for her own staff being drawn down; it was rather like a mother eagle and her cubs.'

From the Westlands incident she lurched into another heart-stopping situation when she sanctioned President Reagan's request to use his F1-11 fighterbombers based at Lakenheath to bomb Colonel Gaddafi's base in Tripoli after another round of Libyan sponsored terrorism which killed an American soldier at a discothèque in Berlin. The President had stood it long enough – he wanted to put an end to the terrorism which had been rocking the free world. Margaret Thatcher, with memories of the Grand Hotel bombing still fresh in her mind, and aware that the IRA drew tremendous financial support and weapons from the Libyans, agreed; above all, she owed a debt to Reagan for his support in the Falklands War.

She paid a high price for the decision – there was total uproar across the country as television broadcasts presented what were, in general, heavily biased reports showing a defenceless Gaddafi and family being staffed by bombs. Gaddafi survived although some members of his family, including an adopted child, did not.

The Prime Minister met a storm of abuse in the House of Commons from members who feared that Britain had become too ready to jump to Reagan's call, and that her decision had been taken with precious little consultation with her colleagues. The public opinion polls indicated the sharp national criticism. Demonstrations appeared at the bases and the Labour and Conservative Parties alike were alarmed. The Conservative popularity reached a new low. It was some time before it became clear that the bombing was justified. Ultimately it did serve the purpose of silencing Gaddafi – since that time his own raids have diminished in number. His support, however, for other terrorist groups did not waver.

Margaret Thatcher's trials and tribulations were still in their infancy. Following quickly in the footsteps of the Westlands affair was a massive row over the discovery that the British-owned car company, Austin Rover, had been involved in talks with

Top, Margaret Thatcher with Jeffrey Archer, 1986. *Bottom*, Deputy Leader Lord Whitelaw at the Conservative Party Central Office.

the American multi-national company, Ford, regarding a possible take-over. Further, the American company General Motors was negotiating to buy the ailing British Leyland truck division. Uproar ensued yet again. The economic factors of a free market were blinkered by emotional allegations that the industry was being sold out to the Americans. Anthony Beaumont-Dark put the feelings into words with his statement that he was 'not prepared to be the pall-bearer at the British motor industry's funeral'. Proposals for British Leyland were withdrawn – an uncharacteristic 'U' turn for the Thatcher Government.

Matters went from bad to worse when the Sunday Trading Bill, initiated by the Conservatives, was blocked and hence sunk, by Margaret Thatcher's own back-bench MPs. To an outsider it might have appeared that she had lost control of her own party. Certainly the country had lost confidence and they hammered it home with the defeat of the Conservative candidate in the seemingly safe Parliamentary seat of Ryedale, where a 16,000 majority was turned over to the Alliance party.

The long winter dragged into a battle-weary summer for the beleaguered Prime Minister. Before she could pause to recapture her strength, South Africa presented itself. The British public were receiving a daily television diet of unattractive extremism by the minority white Government who were locked in an often very bloodied battle against the blacks seeking to end Apartheid and win equal voting rights. No one could fail to be moved by grotesque scenes of violence – white on black and black on black – particularly when accompanied by pictures of 'necklace killings' where black victims accused of collaborating with the whites were attacked with a car tyre filled with burning petrol. An outraged Commonwealth demanded sanctions against the South African Government to starve them economically to defeat.

At this point Margaret Thatcher gathered herself to her full 5 ft 4 in height and said 'NO'. She would not support a course of action which would ultimately cause only greater suffering to the blacks who would be the first to lose their jobs if the white industry collapsed. She also pointed out that sanctions had an inefficient history, and that Britain would also suffer. A British ban on trade with South Africa would put 120,000 British jobs at risk – a fair counterblast to those critical of unemployment at home.

It took a tremendous amount of courage to stand up to such fiery criticism from both the British people and the rest of the Commonwealth. The protesters were angered even more when she pointed out that the black front-line border states would never sustain sanctions, for their own economies were utterly dependent on workers taking jobs in South Africa.

This is damaging publicity hit new heights of influence – causing great harm to her relations with Buckingham Palace. *The Times* reported that the Queen and Prince Philip viewed the South African situation very differently from Thatcher – perhaps because the Commonwealth is the last vestige of real interest that the monarch holds. It is her particular area of influence, and the Queen, as Head of the Commonwealth, felt a personal responsibility for it. She was not amused therefore to see her Prime Minister taking a stand which divided the Commonwealth. It was a case of politics versus the monarchical influence. Public opinion held that a clash with the Queen was the epitome of wrong-doing and in their eyes Margaret Thatcher's standing sank even lower. Embarrassingly she was even booed at Prince Andrew's wedding to Sarah Ferguson, while entertainers like Elton John and Pamela Stephenson were greeted with wild cheering.

And so the hot summer drew on into a burning autumn with the Spycatcher affair at the base of the fire. Peter Wright, a former member of MI5, wrote his autobiography, outlining intimate details of the workings of Britain's security service – material which was clearly in breach of the Official Secrets Act. Margaret Thatcher was appalled – the previously high standards of the Service had been broken down. It would be impossible effectively to run a service whose responsibility was to guard our security if employees were unable to keep to the code of silence. Over the years, dribs and drabs had leaked out through writers like Chapman Pincher and Nigel West. This, however, was the last straw. Peter Wright was, after all, a direct employee and therefore drew upon his head the full legal wrath of Her Majesty's Government. Mrs Thatcher wanted the book banned, and entered a lengthy and high-profile court case in Australia, where Wright lived, to seek those ends. The affair was a nightmare for the Government. They lost on every count and fed the book with an unbelievable amount of publicity.

The price that Margaret Thatcher paid for a principled stance was high. The series of banana skins that had hall-marked her Government of 1983 made clear the message that she could only lose the next General Election. The third force in the country, the Liberal and Social Democratic Alliance, was growing in support as disenchanted Tory voters were focusing their attention on the 'moderates', as they saw them.

But for all her political knocks, one factor remained – Britain was simply booming with prosperity. All the economic agonies of the past had by this time been remedied. Unemployment had dropped dramatically from a high of nearly 4 million to 2 million. More people than ever were in work; more small businesses had grown; output had shot up; and companies were running sleek stream-lined enterprises. As a result, with increased profits and more money to spend, and with videos, computers and other technological instruments creeping into ordinary homes up and down the country, this prosperity had a profound effect on how the electorate would vote in the forthcoming election.

Criticism, they had in plenty, but finally fortune began once more to shine on Margaret Thatcher. She broke free of the unfortunate handcuffs of disasters and made a wildly successful trip to Moscow to meet the then General Secretary, Mikhail Gorbachev. For a start, both Margaret Thatcher and Gorbachev had much to gain by a close working relationship. For the Kremlin it meant they had a third entity whom they understood, trusted and respected, apart from the United States of America. They had recognized that Margaret Thatcher was rapidly becoming the senior statesman for Europe, and astutely realized that she would be around for some time to come.

Margaret Thatcher quickly discovered that she had an important and valid role to play as a buffer statesman between East and West. She also had the experience and the relative youth to continue. Practically speaking, there was an obvious chemistry between the two leaders which fascinated observers. Their relationship had come a long way from the days when *Pravda* had nick-named Margaret Thatcher 'The Iron Lady'. Then, as indeed now, she warned against Soviet military build-up that exceeded mere defence.

She championed vigorously for the deployment of the Cruise and Pershing missiles in the face of the unprovoked and unprecedented deployment of the Soviet SS-20 land-based ballistic missiles targeted on Western Europe. With a token balance now restored she was able to take a look at the ambitious programme of internal reform that Gorbachev had started.

Preparations at Chequers and Downing Street reached a feverous pitch. She had top-level briefings on every possible subject – from the economy to 'Star Wars' and the Soviet's own 'Strategic Defence Initiative' – when experts were flown in from America to aid her. The magic was evident when the two leaders finally met. Margaret

Top, Anti-Thatcher demonstrators in the Midlands during the 1987 Election campaign. *Bottom,* Demonstrators in action during a 1983 Election tour of the South East.

Top, The last official photograph of the 1987 Tory Cabinet. *Centre right*, John Selwyn Gummer with Edwina Currie. *Centre left*, Francis Pym, Foreign Secretary. *Bottom*, Lord Joseph with Lord Young in the House of Lords.

Thatcher was fascinated, while Gorbachev was intensely curious about the woman who had become the first female Prime Minister of Great Britain. They were intellectually equal; they respected one another and their common roles as conviction politicians who had revolutionized their countries.

They entered thirteen hours of talks. Margaret Thatcher was visibly exhilarated – no other Western leader had been given so much time. She stunned not only Gorbachev but also the Soviet nation when she appeared on Soviet television for a full fifty minutes, uncensored – telling the people what she wanted them to know and what for many of them was news: how the West feared the military strength of the Soviet Union.

Margaret Thatcher returned home flushed with pride. She had justified the comment she made about Gorbachev when they first met during his visit to Britain shortly after he had become General Secretary. 'I can do business with this man,' she'd said. That business has now been cemented into a firm, friendly working relationship. It should never, however, be implied that Margaret Thatcher had softened on her views of Communism – or her fears of a Socialist-dominated Britain. The relationship is dynamic and quite different from her relationship with President Reagan. For a start Reagan is a much older man with a gentle and an easy-going charm. Where he could not surpass her intellectual brilliance, he matched her enthusiasm for conviction politics. Like her, Reagan knew his own people – he knew what the man in the street really wanted. He based his agenda on his understanding of the national pulse and his ability to communicate on the same level. Margaret Thatcher admired his sincerity and his beliefs and, let's face it, his charm. He in turn never ceased to wonder and admire this tornado of leadership she embodied – she was unlike anyone he had ever met. His last words to me after a private meeting in the Oval Office at the White House were, 'Give my regards to Mrs Thatcher. She is a very great lady.' It was quite clear that his regard for her had paved the way for me.

Their relationship was open and frank. If Margaret Thatcher felt something was not going smoothly, she never hesitated to telephone; an action never taken more often than in the wake of the Reykjavic Summit with Gorbachev when it appeared that the President had committed himself to a nuclear-free Europe. The record had to be set straight – and she was able to set it without causing offence.

Back home on the domestic scene, the successful trip to Moscow set the tempo for the General Election which would take place on 11 June 1987. From that moment onwards the sky became clearer but for Margaret Thatcher's opponent, Labour's leader Neil Kinnock, it was gloomy. Where she succeeded, he failed dismally. His visit to America in the hope of being hailed as a future leader had flopped. They were not impressed by a man promoting one-sided nuclear disarmament – an ideology that ran contrary to everything they stood for. Kinnock had a bare twelve minutes with the President; there were no enthusiastic crews to meet him; and the final insult was hurled when he arrived at Atlanta to find only a one-man welcome. The man stood patiently at the Arrivals gate, holding up a card saying, 'Kinnock' – he was the cab driver. Things were looking up for the Tories – they'd only just begun to fight.

Margaret Thatcher at the Election Manifesto Press Conference in 1983, outside the Conservative Party Central Office.

CHAPTER TEN
THE 1987 ELECTION

The Labour Party launched a new image for themselves using the rose as their symbol of patriotism. It was a slick well-presented campaign focusing on Kinnock – the warm friendly personality – rather than on substance of policy. Their election campaign got off to a good start; they looked smart and professional. Every day there were photographic opportunities with the press and Neil Kinnock made good headway in his campaign to attract the nation's attention.

The same could not be said for Margaret Thatcher's campaign. Although she was on her third run and should have had an immaculately conceived, prepared and executed campaign, the campaign floundered. It began, however, on a high note: Parliamentary candidates were called to a Birmingham hotel for a briefing by all members of the Cabinet as well as the Prime Minister herself. Her performance was masterly. She was relaxed to the point that she uncharacteristically moved around the platform exploiting the space: she lolled against the desk; folded and unfolded her arms; made grand, sweeping gestures and told triumphant stories of her victory over the tough television inquisitions. She had good reason to be relaxed.

Within days, however, alarm had set in. Against all odds Labour were rising in the polls, the Alliance were sinking and so indeed were the Tories. All was not harmonious within the Tory campaign, beginning with a breakdown of confidence in the Tory Party Chairman, Norman Tebbit, at the end of the first week. Hard on his heels, was Lord Young, a rising star who was brought in to help sort things out. And when the campaign reached 'Wobbly Thursday' she brought in her old friend, Tim Bell, who had played a key role in 1979. Ex-Saatchi & Saatchi, he was working on his own to set the campaign back on course. It was unthinkable that things could go wrong. But suddenly, after months of preparation, it appeared that the campaign lacked punch and direction. It was wooden and paled in comparison with the opportunities being offered visually by Neil Kinnock via television.

The fact that she was consistently cocooned by top security when she moved around did not help nor did it benefit her to continue her practice of having newspapers pre-digested for her. She virtually missed criticisms of her lack-lustre campaign. In effect nobody dared tell her that Central Office had lost their touch.

It was in the end her family who came to the rescue. Carol telephoned her with a stark but anxious warning, 'You'd better get your act together or start packing.' It shocked her mother deeply. She had already guessed privately that her campaign was not up to scratch and was increasingly unhappy about the fact that her first major speech which would take place four days later was still not put together. She immediately called upon her closest advisers for a meeting at No. 10. Apart from Denis, the meeting was attended by Stephen Sherbourne, Lord Young and Tim Bell. The damage was evident;

Top, Margaret Thatcher takes a tea break during the 1987 Election campaign. *Bottom,* Election night victory at Central Office, 1987.

what she wanted was a solution: the next and best step forward. She also needed reassurance, for Margaret Thatcher was more nervous, querulous and fretful than anyone could ever remember seeing her. Her original and successful 1979 campaign team of Cecil Parkinson and Gordon Reece with Alison Wakeham and Caroline Ryder behind the scenes was no longer in charge. The Labour Party had made no bones about it; they were hitting back; portraying the Prime Minister as mean, vicious and harsh with a political programme intended to harm society's weak and poor.

Tim Bell, as a trusted friend, delivered the extent of the news. He outlined where they had gone wrong and built up her confidence. She *would* win. After all, she had a remarkable success story to relate – and bright new promises for the future. Their strategy was to attack. She would hit over and over again at Labour's policies and their hidden or 'Iceberg' Manifesto. She would also modify her personal presentation. After years of slogging it out at the Dispatch Box in the House, against a howling and baying crowd, she now had to make a deliberate effort to soften herself – to become less aggressive and develop a fresh and lively public personality. The tone at the Conservative Party platform had to be lightened.

Their cause was unexpectedly aided by Kinnock himself. In a TV AM interview

Top, Flying in by helicopter, Margaret Thatcher arrives in East Anglia during the 1987 Election tour. *Bottom,* Mrs Thatcher begins her Election campaign at Gatwick Airport.

with David Frost he discussed the issue of armed conflict in Europe for three full minutes. Those precious 180 seconds destroyed his campaign. He admitted that Labour would surrender in the face of defeat brought on by failure to rely on the nuclear deterrent. And in surrender he would rely on guerrilla warfare to make any occupation totally untenable.

From that moment onwards he could do no right. The Tories put out an advertisement showing a soldier with his hands up and the slogan 'Labour's Policy on Arms'.

In the final week of the campaign it was decided that her campaigning day should be very slightly eased. For a woman of sixty-one she was still tearing around

Top, Margaret Thatcher sits in the driver's seat of the Conservative bus in the Docklands. *Bottom,* Denis Thatcher downs a glass of beer during a visit to a Glasgow brewery. Margaret looks on with amusement.

on a twenty-hour day. In the past it had been acceptable but she was beginning to tire. The final week was the most co-ordinated of the campaign; Cecil Parkinson was brought back to be by her side. They began to concentrate on the fear issues: a Labour Government would bring back strikes; industrial strife; inflation; hostility towards law and order and the police; and they would be fuelled by impossibly high spending plans and taxation.

In return Labour hit back with personal abuse and interviews accusing her of 'not caring'. This last attack did hurt; it hurt her deeply and she talked frequently about it in private to her colleagues. She desperately wanted to reply. It was *because* of her caring that she wanted to tackle inflation, trade unions, the Falklands, the miners and unemployment. Admittedly it was wise for her not to dwell on the structural plans the Tories had for the welfare state and the health service. It was not a time to spill proposals unnecessarily, although Labour tried to push her into doing so.

She carried on with her message through television interviews, and on the road. Only days before Polling Day she broke off the campaign to attend the Economic Summit in Venice, using it as a platform on which to demonstrate her policies. She received their plaudits in return. She was the acknowledged leader of the West. She arrived home to prepare the final speeches, agonizingly constructed as always. More than ever before she crammed in television and radio appearances as well as rally speeches. The air space she received was staggering. The campaign depended on her energies right up to the final moment, but fatigue was beginning to set in. 'Rather than cancel anything I would have crawled on that stage and missed it if need be.' Without a doubt this combined blitz of interviews pulled the campaign to success.

After all the heartache and earlier disorganization, harmony was returned. In a quiet moment later in the afternoon of Polling Day, the tour of her constituency completed, Margaret Thatcher called Norman Tebbit at Central Office. He came over and spent over two and a half hours with her. Despite some earlier tension they have always had a warm regard for each other. She had enormous admiration for his talents in the Cabinet and in Cabinet committees and, in short, his political feel. As far as she was concerned she wanted him to continue. But no, he told her gently that he had a duty to his wife, Margaret. She needed round the clock attention and moral support. He felt now that he owed it to her to be close at hand – he would return to the back benches.

The evening wore on. At 2.30 a.m. her results were announced in Finchley – she'd won her constituency. She went back to Central Office – when she left for Downing Street at 5.30 a.m. her majority had been assured. Forty-four per cent of the first time voters had supported the Tories. Unfortunately, they had lost eleven of the twenty-one Conservative seats in Scotland.

With only an hour's sleep she was up and ready to go. It was time to form her third Conservative Government.

It was a feat indeed. The campaign may have had its low moments, but despite those factors victory was theirs. The electorate voted unequivocally for Margaret Thatcher. They had done well by her and they knew it. Eighty-seven per cent of the

Top right, Margaret and Denis Thatcher outside the Finchley Conservative Party headquarters. *Top Left*, Denis and Margaret casting an early vote at their polling station in London. *Bottom right*, Flag-waving Margaret Thatcher in Newport, Gwent. *Bottom left*, 'We shall win,' says Margaret Thatcher outside the polling station.

population's standard of living was rising and it would keep rising. And what was made abundantly clear was the fact that neither Margaret Thatcher nor her party had run out of steam. There were plenty of radical policies to come – shaping Britain for the 1990s and beyond.

It all boiled down to a basic philosophy. As Margaret Thatcher said, 'It's a mixture of fundamentally sound economics. You live within your means; you have honest money, therefore you don't make reckless promises. You recognize human nature is such that it needs incentives to work harder, so you cut your tax. It's about being worth while and honourable. And about the family.

'And about that is something which is rather unique and enterprising in the British character – it's about how we built an Empire and how we gave sound administration and sound law to large areas of the world. All those things are still there in the British people, aren't they?'

Well, aren't they?

Norman Tebbit and Cecil Parkinson enthusiastically confirm the victory.

CHAPTER ELEVEN
THE LATER YEARS

Margaret Thatcher had attained her third election victory. Not since Lord Liverpool won three consecutive elections between 1812 and 1827 had a British Prime Minister accomplished such a dazzling feat. Thatcherism had hit its mark. Margaret Thatcher would only modestly admit that she happened to be the vehicle for a new political philosophy. It may be true that luck played its part, that timing too had a role – but no philosophy can be given life without a dynamic push from its source. Margaret Thatcher lived and breathed her philosophy and that became its very strength. Her 'commitment' and drive rose above the personal abuse and criticism her philosophy attracted. Perhaps that is what made it work. She had a clear vision and, never having been one to seek personal popularity, was in a position to see it through.

Resting on her laurels has never been Margaret Thatcher's style. The third term represented a chance to get on with the parts of the programme that she had not yet been able to complete or tackle. Her very successes in the economy had invited their own criticism. As spending power increased, so did the jibes from the Labour Party. 'It's the "loadsamoney" syndrome,' they cried. 'This is a materialist, selfish, greedy society.'

In 1988, back in Brighton for the first time since the IRA bombing of the Grand Hotel, Margaret Thatcher shot back firmly, 'Prosperity has created not the selfish society but the generous society . . . Personal effort doesn't undermine the community; it enhances the community. When individual talents are held back, the community is held back too.'

She was also back to fight Socialism – her commitment to her cause beliefs never waning. It was no good having adventurous, novel Tory policies unless everyone for whom they are destined can benefit. She was determined that no corner in the land would go without every individual having his chance. 'We have to help those families. Otherwise they'll be browbeaten by Socialist councillors and bombarded by Socialist propaganda, calculated to deny them the opportunities we have provided.'

But of course every success has its price: the boom economy gave rise to borrowing – even credit card borrowing reached a high. Britain was ordering more goods from abroad than she was exporting and the net result was a substantial trade deficit. The borrowing had to be paid for. In the Autumn of 1987, the Chancellor of the Exchequer, Nigel Lawson, raised interest rates. Some said it was a crisis – the Government had stumbled after all. Margaret Thatcher and her team at No. 10 were calm. They felt sure that a steadying hand on borrowing and controlling inflation – which had arisen out of a too successful boom – was the answer – there would be no lasting damage.

After all, Britain's last bout of high inflation had been a result of Callaghan's spending spree on Government-spending programmes – using funds that Britain did not have. This time the borrowing came from the private sector whose very successes gave rise to their spending power and created a boom time for credit card companies.

There was still work to be done on law and order, one of the fundamental platforms of the Conservative party. Ironically, prosperity had not reduced violence, contrary to the Labour view that violence grows out of inner city deprivation and unemployment. Although deprivation was becoming obsolete, society was still violent. The fighting by British fans at Belgium's Heysal stadium in which forty-three Italian fans were crushed to death horrified and shamed the Prime Minister. She had already supported her Home Secretary, Douglas Hurd, in his efforts to raise police numbers – their pay and powers. She introduced measures to control fans carrying knives and firearms – they would be stopped and searched before entry.

And if muggings, knifings and sheer thuggery by the lager louts were not enough, another form of violence had publicly shown its head – after generations of being an unspoken deviation, child abuse had become a subject of national debate. Her message on the subject left no grey areas. 'Anyone who commits violence against a child should have no shred of doubt about the severity of the sentence for that sort of brutality.'

Not surprisingly Margaret Thatcher has always felt somewhat bitter at the poor support she has received from the opposition in fighting violence. There were some areas like defence, and law and order, where a common agreement had always abounded. Now that is no longer the case. In particular she has always found it very hard to forgive the Labour Party for obstructing her attempts to fight terrorism. They refused to support the Prevention of Terrorism Act – an act which has been vital to the impending defeat of the IRA and indeed has saved so many lives.

Bad feeling rose to a feverish pitch when she was criticized for sanctioning the SAS to fly into Gibraltar and shoot three IRA terrorists who were planning to bomb a regular Tuesday parade on the Rock: hundreds would have been killed or injured. As it was the terrorists were stopped in their tracks. The opposition cried that they should have been simply arrested – why kill them? The Government response was that in essence these people had been shooting to kill innocent people for years. They had to be judged and dealt with in their own manner – they had simply never understood or lived by normal codes of law and democracy and, for that matter, morality. Similarly, international relations took a plunge during the 'Father' Patrick Ryan case. Her fight against terrorism would not allow her any half-measured response. Her fury dominated the European Community Summit in Rhodes.

Margaret Thatcher's promise to seek a better relationship with the Eastern bloc took on a new impetus during the autumn of 1988. For months Margaret Thatcher had been planning her trip to Poland. Her visit held only one provision – she wanted to meet with Solidarity, visit Gdansk and have talks with Lech Walesa. It was a tribute to her forcefulness and determination that the Jaruzelski regime allowed her this freedom. The response from the beleaguered Poles was overwhelming. She was mobbed wherever she went, a situation not seen on Polish television but freely shown in the West. The climax came when she attended a packed Roman Catholic church

Top, Mrs Thatcher has forgotten a hairclip in her anticipation of meeting the Chinese Prime Minister Chou en Lai. *Bottom,* The Chinese Prime Minister arrives at Kensington Gardens.

where she was greeted with heartfelt singing and flowers. Pictures showed her visibly moved as tears welled up in her eyes. In short, it was a triumphant visit – and a big step forward for human rights.

Back home she plunged into a whirl of arrangements to visit Washington and establish a working rapport with the President-elect George Bush – and take a moment to say goodbye to President Reagan, who laid on a farewell banquet in the White House where he danced for the last time as President with Margaret. Denis took Nancy to the floor. Their tributes to one another were warm and effusive. For Mr Bush who was looking on, it would undoubtedly be a hard act to follow.

The morning after the banquet, Margaret Thatcher met with Bush. It seemed, at first, as if the 'gelling' would take some time. George Bush is conscious that he must make his own mark – and also aware of the fact that Margaret Thatcher is determined

Top, Margaret Thatcher speaks to HRH Prince Philip, and HM The Queen addresses assembled military leaders as they wait at Windsor for the arrival of the Dubai Leader. *Bottom right*, Margaret and Denis leave the Grand Hotel in Brighton for the Agents' dinner and dance. *Bottom left*, HM The Queen Mother arrives at No. 10 for a dinner in honour of her 80th birthday.

to set her own stamp on international relations. She suggested a Summit of Western leaders in London to coincide with the NATO ministerial meeting in June, and although the idea was initially put to one side, a month later the suggestion was taken on. The Summit, hosted by Margaret Thatcher, would be a truly fitting crown to her first decade in office, coming at a time when NATO would celebrate its fortieth anniversary.

Now, more than ever, Margaret Thatcher is acutely aware that time will not stand still for the West – the relationship of Britain and the West with the Soviet Union is rapidly changing. Gorbachev, a man Margaret Thatcher feels she understands, has been studying the intricacies of the propaganda war, and many complex messages are coming out of the Soviet Union. In 1988 and 1989, the public had been exposed to more news than ever from the Soviet Union, whether it was examinations on the progress of *perestroika* and *glasnost* or news of the troubles arising from the outlying republics seeking independence. Without doubt this raised public sympathy has led to Gorbachev's being rated as the most admired leader in the world.

From the difficult standpoint of seeking better relations and at the same time pushing the Soviets to live up to their promise of publishing their armed forces figures, and making real cuts in their superiority in conventional forces including chemical weapons, there has had to be some fast footwork.

Whatever the public sympathies may be with the Soviet Union, Margaret Thatcher has always been acutely aware that they still spend 17 per cent of their GDP on defence – a sum far in excess of needs and way beyond anything NATO spends. The sums also indicate a fearsome military strength, a fact that she has been aware of throughout negotiations – thus her stance on NATO's modernization programme. As the next decade evolves, public attention will be focused again on NATO's conventional and nuclear weapon resolutions.

Public perception of the Soviet threat diminished further when Armenia was destroyed by an earthquake which devastated an entire region and killed an estimated 200,000 people, leaving many more thousands injured and homeless. The sheer scale of the tragedy brought rescue teams and messages expressing sympathy and shock from around the world. After a supremely successful visit to the United Nations in New York where Gorbachev had spoken of the Soviet Union's commitment to

Four past and present Conservative Prime Ministers. Sir Alec Douglas Home, Mrs Margaret Thatcher, Edward Heath and The Earl of Stockton.

withdraw one-sidedly 10,000 tanks and 500,000 men from its eastern borders, Gorbachev had been scheduled to pass through London for talks with Margaret Thatcher and tea with the Queen at Buckingham Palace. The news of the earthquake was broken to Gorbachev during a lunch with Reagan and Bush. Early estimates did not reveal the sheer extent of the disaster; however, as the day drew to a close Gorbachev decided to cut short his overseas visit and return straight home.

At 6 a.m. the next morning, BBC Radio 4's *Today* programme announced that Gorbachev would not after all be visiting Margaret Thatcher. Within minutes the studios received a telephone call, 'This is Margaret of Westminster – a first-time caller,' said a powerful voice. And as an aside to an assistant, the stunned interviewer (after a momentary splutter of 'No, no I can handle this myself', to an equally excited assistant) found himself on the air with his Prime Minister with no time to prepare himself for questions.

'This is the very first I have heard of it. I want you to know I totally sympathize with Mr Gorbachev. Of course he must go back to his people,' Margaret Thatcher said during the impromptu interview. And with that she set in motion an immediate relief programme. The largest spontaneous donation from any country, she sent £5 million in hard currency as a start and took the opportunity to encourage the British people to donate anything they could. In turn it is interesting to note that the Soviet Union allowed their plight to be publicly recorded as well as accepting foreign assistance.

Previous page, **P**rime Minister Margaret Thatcher and Soviet Leader Mikhail Gorbachev during their talks at RAF Brize-Norton. (*Press Association*). *Above,* With Mr Bill Bailey, the England Mascot, at the Bournemouth Conference.

Top, Margaret Thatcher leaving Brighton after the 1988 Party Conference. *Bottom*, Victory celebration at the Conservative Party Conference, 1988.

In the long term, this horrific tragedy may have acted as a bond for the two leaders and the two countries. There is still, however, much ground to be covered and naturally all negotiations will be approached with the traditional caution. Margaret Thatcher, while announcing friendship and giving every possible help she could, was and is under no illusions about the fact that the Soviet Union is a Marxist-Leninist state, ultimately intent on making itself more powerful and more influential in world affairs. Indeed, Margaret Thatcher has never been under any illusions about the strength of Socialism. She told a private farewell party for the retiring Central Office agent Sir Anthony Garner, 'There is a great deal more work to do, despite three successful election wins. Socialism is not dead.'

Top, **D**enis and Margaret Thatcher visit a factory in the Midlands during the 1983 Election tour. *Bottom*, Margaret takes the opportunity to relax in the fields of Sussex.

Top, Prime Minister raises three fingers to signal her third election victory. Norman Tebbit (right) smiles approvingly. *Bottom right,* Margaret Thatcher addresses a 1987 Press Conference at the Conservative Central Office in London. *Bottom left,* Margaret makes friends with a Guide Dog for the Blind in Devon during the 1987 Election tour.

Ever conscious of the havoc she had seen Socialism cause to her own society, encouraging near anarchy from minority groups, she was anxious that Europe should not go headlong down the route of international Socialism. With this in mind she headed for Bruges where she spoke about Britain's, or rather her, views for the future. She was in her element. She looked marvellously chic and confident, arguing forcefully against a federalized Europe. The Socialist Europeans were enraged, as she herself admitted, 'It caused a bit of a stir. Indeed, from some of the reactions you would have thought I had re-opened the Hundred Years War.'

The European Community's move towards 1992 called for the completion of the market barrier breakdown and Margaret Thatcher warned against new ambitions that would include a Europe governed by Socialist methods, and with centralized control and regulation. She noted, 'Well, we haven't worked all these years to free Britain from the paralysis of Socialism only to see it creep in through the back door of central control and bureaucracy from Brussels.'

It was a firm statement and in the long term privately welcomed, for no country was really willing to surrender its sovereignty. But a clear statement had been required and it took someone who had become a senior statesman in Europe to make it.

The future of Britain is very much a focal point of Margaret Thatcher's current thought. She wishes not just to push through outstanding Government business like the restructuring of the rates through the community charge or the restructuring of the health service, but to set a platform and way of life which will be hard to reverse. Inevitably Britain will be playing a closer and more active role in European economics and politics, and with the status, the sense of direction, and above all the economic

The Prime Minister makes a point.

Top, Margaret Thatcher address the CBI Conference at the Albert Hall, London. *Bottom*, With Ronald Reagan at the House of Commons.

strength that Britain has developed, it is a nation that will be heard. The challenges of a changing world – in which Britain's great ally, the United States of America, is re-examining her own position, weakened by a serious national debt causing the country to become somewhat introspective – are enormous.

Margaret Thatcher's epitaph, if she has ever thought of one, would certainly be the fact that she has firmly set Britain's agenda for the future. Thatcherism may evolve and even modify as the next decade passes. With good health for both herself and Denis, perhaps she will choose to run for another term. Even then she will be only in her mid-sixties – quite able to carry out her ideas with characteristic enthusiasm and determination.

The day will come when Margaret Thatcher acknowledges the time to retire. Her mission will be complete: She will gracefully hand over the baton – there can be no doubt. But as she has said, 'I shall hate leaving No. 10, but eventually, of course, I shall.'

And when she does move on, her legacy will have been profound; a new Britain has arisen with a new confidence and a new influence. In short, as she noted, 'What I did was restore Britain.'

She restored Britain – and by doing so unconsciously became its new *Boadicea*. The ordinary man's battle has been fought and won. She has become more than a politician. Today she is a statesman with that extra regal touch. She epitomizes a success story – an unprivileged woman who has become the personification of Britannia. Man will remember her victories. She is now accorded with the highest accolade – she has superseded Churchill and de Gaulle both in personality and in her sense of mission to her people.

Prime Minister Margaret Thatcher poses for Srdja Djukanovic's exclusive shots in her sitting room at No. 10 Downing Street, 1988.

AND INTO THE NINETIES

And what does the future hold for Margaret Thatcher? Certainly she plans to retire at some point and for years there has been speculation regarding the next leader. Sir Geoffrey Howe, Kenneth Baker, Douglas Hurd and Cecil Parkinson have all been potential nominees for the premiership. Even the brilliant, but somewhat erratic, Michael Hesseltine has been placed among the contenders. But the fact remains – Margaret Thatcher is still in her prime and undoubtedly she will lead the Conservative Party into the next General Election in 1991. Tory insiders suspect that she will be tempted to see in the millennium celebrations before she succumbs to retirement.

Margaret Thatcher has led the country in a new direction and political forces have taken on new focus. By the next election, opposition parties will undoubtedly have re-established themselves, shedding the prehistoric Socialist policies that have prohibited their popularity. When new and more dynamic politicians filter into the opposition – politicians who are able to work within a capitalist, thriving Britain – only then will Britain be ready to accept a new form of government. For Margaret Thatcher and Thatcherism itself have turned the tide and pride of Britain. Her philosophies, albeit often controversial, have proved that Britain can flourish.

Many of her policies are still in adolescence, and as the last decade has proved, good things *do* come to those who wait; prosperity has sprung from hardship. The nation is not ready for a new leader – Britain lies curious *and* confident of the changes that are destined to make her even greater. Until Margaret Thatcher's strategies and visions have been realized, she will continue to capture the imaginations and votes of the electorate.

One woman has unwaveringly led Britain back to the forefront of international politics; one woman has restored prosperity and pride. Margaret Thatcher has led a revolution based on Victorian values and a strong belief in the personal potential of every man and woman. She is destined to evoke more controversy and criticism as she surges forth into the future, but the fact remains – she's still here and Thatcherism was born to survive.